BEAUTY

Beauty challenges conventional approaches to the subject through an interdisciplinary approach that forges connections between the arts, sciences and mathematics. Classical, conventional aspects of beauty are addressed in subtle, unexpected ways: symmetry in mathematics, attraction in the animal world and beauty in the cosmos. This collection arises from the Darwin College Lecture Series of 2011 and includes essays from eight distinguished scholars, all of whom are held in esteem not only for their research but also for their ability to communicate their subject to popular audiences. Each essay is entertaining, accessible and thought-provoking and is accompanied by images illustrating beauty in practice.

THE DARWIN COLLEGE LECTURES

These essays are developed from the 2011 Darwin College Lecture Series. Now in their twenty-seventh year, these popular Cambridge talks take a single theme each year. Internationally distinguished scholars, skilled as popularisers, address the theme from the point of view of eight different arts and sciences disciplines.

Subjects covered in the series include

THE DARWIN COLLEGE LECTURES

Beauty

Edited by *Lauren Arrington*, *Zoë Leinhardt* and *Philip Dawid*

CAMBRIDGE
UNIVERSITY PRESS

University Printing House, Cambridge CB2 8BS, United Kingdom

Published in the United States of America by Cambridge University Press, New York

Cambridge University Press is part of the University of Cambridge.

It furthers the University's mission by disseminating knowledge in the pursuit of education, learning and research at the highest international levels of excellence.

www.cambridge.org
Information on this title: www.cambridge.org/9781107693432

© Darwin College, 2013

First published 2013

A catalogue record for this publication is available from the British Library

Library of Congress Cataloguing in Publication data
Beauty / edited by Lauren Arrington, Zoë Leinhardt, Philip Dawid.
  pages cm. – (Darwin College lectures)
Includes bibliographical references and index.
ISBN 978-1-107-69343-2 (Paperback)
 1. Aesthetics. I. Arrington, Lauren, 1981- editor of compilation. II. Leinhardt, Zoë, editor of compilation. III. Dawid, Philip, editor of compilation.
BH39.B3824 2013
1110.85–dc23 2012036780

ISBN 978-1-107-69343-2 Paperback

Additional resources for this publication at www.cambridge.org/9781107693432

Contents

Notes on contributors

Jeanne Altmann is a behavioural ecologist with focus on the life-history of natural populations of long-lived and highly social primates. This empirical research involves almost daily data collection on the Amboseli population of baboons, now four decades and seven generations deep (see www.princeton. edu/~baboon). She has served on various external advisory boards, currently including the Wisconsin National Primate Research Center, the Max Planck Institute for Evolutionary Anthropology in Leipzig and the Institute of Primate Research of the National Museums of Kenya. She was previously Professor and Chair of the Committee on Evolutionary Biology at the University of Chicago and is currently Eugene Higgins Professor Emeritus in Princeton's Department of Ecology and Evolutionary Biology, a faculty associate in Princeton's Office of Population Research and the Princeton Environmental Institute, and an honorary lecturer at the University of Nairobi, Kenya. She is a member of the US National Academy of Sciences.

Carolin Crawford is an astronomer at the Institute of Astronomy in Cambridge, and a Fellow of Emmanuel College, Cambridge. Her research focuses on the properties of the most massive galaxies in the universe, using data collected from the largest ground-based and space telescopes. Carolin combines her research and teaching with her other passion – communicating her love of astronomy to as wide an audience as possible. She runs the outreach programme at the Institute of Astronomy and, in addition to giving many talks on a wide range of astronomical topics, is a regular contributor to both national and local radio programmes. In 2009 Carolin was noted as one of the UKRC's Women of Outstanding Achievement for the communication of science with a contribution to society. (See www-xray.ast.cam.ac.uk/~csc/.)

Evgeny A. Dobrenko is Professor and Head of the Department of Russian and Slavonic Studies of the University of Sheffield. He is the author, editor or co-editor of twenty books, and has published more than 250 articles and essays on Soviet cultural and intellectual history, literature, film, visual arts, architecture, photography, media and music, Socialist Realism and critical theory, which have been translated into eight languages. His books include the monographs *Stalinist Cinema and the Production of History: Museum of the Revolution* (2008), *Political Economy of Socialist Realism* (2007) and *Aesthetics of Alienation: Reassessment of Early Soviet Cultural Theories* (2005).

José Hernández alternates his studies between the Spanish Institute and the French School in Tangiers. He enjoys long-distance running and draws relentlessly. He exhibited his first works at the Librairie des Colonnes in Tangiers in 1962 and in 1964 settled in Madrid. There, he presented his first solo exhibition in 1966 at Galería Edurne. In 1967 he published his first etchings and lithographs. His work as an engraver, which complements his painting, has resulted in several books in collaboration with writers. He has also worked as an illustrator. Since 1974 he has collaborated in a number of theatrical projects as a stage and costume designer for both classic and contemporary plays. At present, he is a voted-in member of the Real Academia de Bellas Artes de San Fernando in Madrid, has been awarded the Honorary Medal of the Real Academia de Bellas Artes de Santa Isabel de Hungría in Seville, and is a member of the European Academy of Sciences, Fine Arts and Literature in Paris.

Jason C. Kuo is Professor of Art History and Archaeology at the University of Maryland, College Park. He studied connoisseurship at the National Palace Museum and later received his Ph.D. from the University of Michigan, Ann Arbor, and has taught at Williams College and Yale University. His recent books and exhibition catalogues include *Practising Art History and Art Criticism* (2002); *Transforming Traditions in Modern Chinese Painting: Huang Pin-hung's Late Work* (2004), and *Chinese Ink Painting Now* (2010). His honours include an Andrew W. Mellon Foundation Fellowship, a grant from the National Endowment for the Humanities, two Stoddard Fellowships in Asian Art at the Detroit Institute of Arts, and two fellowships from the J. D. Rockefeller III Fund. In 1991–2 he received the Lilly Fellowship for teaching excellence at the University of Maryland.

Elizabeth Eva Leach is Professor of Music at the University of Oxford and a Fellow of St Hugh's College, Oxford. She is the author of *Sung Birds: Music, Nature, and Poetry in the Later Middle Ages* (2007), and has broad interests in song, music, music theory and literature. Her monograph entitled *Guillaume de Machaut: Secretary, Poet, Musician* was published in 2011.

Robert McCredie May, Lord May of Oxford, OM AC Kt FRS, holds a professorship at Oxford University and is a Fellow of Merton College, Oxford. He was President of the Royal Society (2000–5) and before that Chief Scientific Adviser to the UK Government and Head of the UK Office of Science and Technology (1995–2000). His career includes a Personal Chair in Physics at Sydney University aged thirty-three, Class of 1877 Professor of Zoology at Princeton, and in 1988 a move to Britain as Royal Society Research Professor. His honours include the Royal Swedish Academy's Crafoord Prize, the Swiss–Italian Balzan Prize, the Japanese Blue Planet Prize, and the Royal Society's Copley Medal, its oldest (1731) and most prestigious award.

Frank Wilczek is Herman Feshbach Professor of Physics at MIT. He has made foundational contributions to several areas of theoretical physics. His work has been recognized with many honours, including the Nobel Prize in 2004. He has written and lectured extensively for non-specialist audiences, and won prizes for that too.

Lauren Arrington is Lecturer in Literature at the Institute of Irish Studies, University of Liverpool. She was Adrian Research Fellow in English at Darwin College from 2008 to 2009, during which time she completed the monograph, *W. B. Yeats, the Abbey Theatre, Censorship, and the Irish State: Adding the Half-Pence to the Pence* (2010), based on her Oxford D.Phil. Her research is focused on twentieth-century literature and history, particularly the areas of Modernism, anti-imperialist writing and life writing.

Zoë Malka Leinhardt is a planetary astrophysicist researching the formation of planets. Her interest in the beauty of physics and mathematics emerged when she was thirteen years old and made a series of photographs of lasers and dry ice. She is currently an STFC Advanced Fellow in the School of Physics at the University of Bristol. At the time of the lecture series she was a Research Fellow at Darwin College and an STFC Postdoctoral Fellow in the Department of Applied Mathematics and Theoretical Physics at the University of Cambridge.

Philip Dawid is a Fellow of Darwin College and Professor of Statistics at Cambridge University. He holds the Snedecor Award for Best Publication in Biometry, the DeGroot Prize for a Published Book in Statistical Science, and the Royal Statistical Society's Guy Medals in Bronze and Silver. His research interests focus on general principles of reasoning from evidence, both statistical evidence and more general forms, including legal and forensic evidence. He was joint editor of a recent book, *Evidence, Inference and Enquiry*, that resulted from an interdisciplinary research programme he had directed at University College London.

Figures

Introduction

Beauty, truth and the sublime

In December 1817 John Keats wrote to his brothers, George and Tom, after dining with the English artist William Hayden: 'The excellence of every Art is its intensity, capable of making all disagreeables evaporate, from their being in close relationship with Beauty & Truth.'[1] Two years later, Hayden's articles on Classical and medieval art, published in the *Examiner* in May 1819, inspired Keats's 'Ode on a Grecian Urn' in which the poet famously gives the 'Attic shape' words to comfort man: 'Beauty is truth, truth beauty, – that is all/ Ye know on earth, and all ye need to know.'[2] The Modernist poet T. S. Eliot dismissed Keats's equation of truth and beauty as 'meaningless', but scholarship in science and mathematics holds fast to the accuracy of Keats's assertion.[3] The simplicity of the equation, which was so objectionable to Eliot, reflects the Classical search for purity of form, which produced the beautifully clear mathematics of Pythagoras and Euclid that Frank Wilczek and Bob May celebrate here in their chapters, 'Quantum beauty' and 'Beauty and truth'.

If 'beauty is truth' then beauty cannot be purely pleasurable. Yet if the intensity of a work of art is sufficient, Keats argues, it enables the subject to transcend its 'disagreeable' elements and provide access to truth through the observer's experience of the sublime. As W. P. Albrecht

---

[1] Quoted in William Walsh, *Introduction to Keats* (London: Methuen, 1981), 77.
[2] John Keats, 'Ode on a Grecian Urn' in *John Keats: Poems*, selected by Andrew Motion (London: Faber, 2000), 65–6.
[3] Martin Gardner, 'Is Beauty Truth and Truth Beauty? How Keats's Famous Line Applies to Math and Science', *Scientific American* (18 March 2007), www.scientificamerican.com/article.cfm?id=is-beauty-truth-and-truth (accessed 30 October 2011).

explains in 'The Tragic Sublime of Hazlitt and Keats', the sublime for these writers was not the delightful horror of Edmund Burke and William Wordsworth, to which Evgeny Dobrenko refers in his chapter, 'Terror by beauty'. Keats defined the sublime as a moment in which the 'imagination excited by passion ... selects and combines sensory details to catch the "verisimilitude" which an object or experience has for him at that moment'.[4] For the artist José Hernández, beauty is something that can be manifested in the external world once the imagination has done its work, both in the process of creation and perception: a process that he explores in his chapter on the relationship between 'Beauty and the grotesque'. The tensions amid beauty, truth and the sublime are interrogated by all of the contributors to this volume. In his discussion, Bob May finds Keats's equation pleasing but problematic since 'the overriding precept for Truth in science is that an ugly fact trumps a beautiful theory', to which Hernández unwittingly replies, 'Is ugly the opposite of beautiful, perhaps, or that which does not fit in with the infallible formula of a given concept or precept?'

Keats thus proves insufficient for our study of beauty and can be complemented fruitfully by the philosophy of Immanuel Kant, which incorporates reason into the imaginative process: 'the imagination must succeed in representing these [visible] forms to the understanding' if beauty is to be perceived.[5] And so we have May's assertion that the simplicity of beauty is best understood in large-scale mathematical models of complex patterns, which enable us to understand 'how the real world actually works' and Wilczek's attention to the quantum world, which – invisible to the eye – is perceptible through imagination and reason working together to create beautiful models, Platonic shadows, that show us the truth of the world imagined in ancient Greece.

These essays confirm Kant's aesthetic in that they demonstrate the way in which our experience of beauty must be mediated by laws of nature or social convention. Elizabeth Eva Leach opens her chapter, 'The sound of beauty', with a discussion of the song of the sirens, the beauty

---

[4] W. P. Albrecht, 'The Tragic Sublime of Hazlitt and Keats', repr. as 'The Poetry of John Keats' in Harold Bloom (ed.), *The Sublime* (New York: Bloom's Literary Criticism, 2010), 119.

[5] Albrecht, 'Tragic Sublime', 111.

of which Odysseus could only experience within constraints. Leach suggests that this chimes with St Augustine's assertion that a rational theoretical framework was essential to the perception of music versus sound and to aesthetic appreciation versus base enjoyment. Was Augustine's nightingale an inspiration for Keats's ode to that 'immortal Bird' whose voice 'was heard/In ancient days by emperor and clown'?[6]

The experience of beauty and the sublime relies on structure – and, inversely, beauty and the sublime have been used as tools to disguise repressive structures. Drawing from a strain of intellectual history separate from and more dominant than Keats's conception of the sublime, Dobrenko argues that 'Beauty cannot be conceived without truth ... But the sublime is indifferent to truth'. On the basis of this theoretical framework, we can comprehend the totalitarian endorsement of grandiose architectural projects that functioned as tangible symbols of the resurrection of ancient civilizations or the creation of futuristic utopias; the sublimation of the anxiety of repressed individuals through membership of mass categories; and the cult of the leader that creates a secular divinity to replace the terror of the supernaturally divine.

The discomfort provoked by encounters with the raw power of the totalitarian sublime is closely related to the repulsion humans experience when confronted with behaviour that is not sublimated by culture. Jeanne Altmann's chapter on 'Beauty and attraction' begins by interrogating the reasons for our aversion to observing our sexual behaviour mirrored by primates, whose physical features and social habits are so closely related to our own. Building on over forty years of fieldwork in Kenya and the observation of seven generations of a baboon family group, she discusses theories of attraction through various social bonds, from sexual partners to the reception (and rejection) of infants by social groups, juvenile friendships, and adult grooming behaviour. Altmann's subtitle, 'in the "eye" of the beholder', is multivalent since it points to the human relationship to other animal species and the centrality of relativity and flux to social bonds. The biological information that dictates animal behaviour varies over a lifetime and with it conceptions of beauty and attraction.

***

[6] 'Ode to a Nightingale' in *John Keats: Poems*, 67–9.

The relativity of beauty and the role of artifice is Jason Kuo's theme in 'Beauty and happiness'. He suggests that Western conceptions of beauty have often impeded an appreciation of Chinese art, yet his discussion of the importance of calligraphy in Chinese painting raises themes that are familiar from the preceding chapters in this volume, which draw heavily from ancient Greece. The painter of bamboo, for example, 'must have the perfected bamboo in mind'; beauty can only be achieved by spontaneity once the traditional skill has been mastered. From a tradition distinct from Western culture, we hear resonances of the Platonic forms and of Kant's emphasis on the necessity of structured reason ('understanding') alongside the imaginative impulse. Perhaps we are closer to a universal conception of beauty than we think.

Carolin Crawford's chapter, which concludes this volume, shows us beauty on a scale that eclipses civilizations and species. Her explanation of the life cycle of stars and the science of nebulae is a beautifully simple articulation of the complex structures of our universe. Our understanding of star formations that dwarf our solar system can but bring us into proximity with beauty and the sublime in all its passion and terror.

In our endeavour to explore the diversity of beauty, commonalities have arisen serendipitously. The sequence of essays that follows reflects exactly the order of the Darwin College Lecture Series of 2011, when the audience heard a question posed in one week and answered in another, themes introduced by allusion then taken up in full. We would like to thank each of the lecturers for their sensitive, rigorous approach to beauty and their enthusiastic participation in the series, which can be revisited in this volume and online at www.sms.cam.ac.uk/collection/1093580. We would like to thank the Master, William Brown; the Vice-Master, Andy Fabian; the Education and Research Committee and the Fellows of the College for supporting our theme. The Master's Secretary, Janet Gibson, devoted long hours and her own time to the series, and, without her work, *Beauty* would not have been a success. The College Art Committee, particularly Margaret Cone and Alan Blackwell, and the Clerk of Works, Philip Waterson, and the Deputy Clerk of Works, Clive Taylor, were indispensable in preparing the exhibition in College, which also would not have been possible without the support of the Bursar, Peter Brindle. The Butler, Ian Smith, was wonderfully flexible in extending the reception

to 1 Newnham Terrace. Espen Koht, Tony Cox and Markus Kalberer provided vital technical acumen for which the speakers and we are very grateful. Zoë Leinhardt would like to thank her husband, Andrew Young, for taking care of her son while she was travelling to Cambridge every week. We would like to thank the Director of the Fitzwilliam Museum, Timothy Potts, and the Head of Education at the museum, Julia Tozer, for their collaboration in the Beauty Walk and their publicity of the series. Jessie Hohmann played an integral role in organizing the series and tackled the difficult task of negotiating rights for reproduction. We would like to thank the following for permission to reproduce the images that are included in this book: the Newberry Library, Chicago; the Bodleian Library, Oxford; the Vendôme Library; the Digital Image Archive of Medieval Music; the Palace Museum, Taiwan; Frank Wilczek's assistant, Charles Suggs; and José Hernández. Thomas Hövel's freeware program, WinCIG, was used to create the images in figures 1.6–1.9. For colour versions of some of the images appearing in the volume, see www.darwin. cam.ac.uk/beauty/lectures. Every effort has been made to trace copyright holders and we apologise for any unintentional omissions.
Lauren Arrington
Zoë Malka Leinhardt
Philip Dawid

1 Beauty and truth: their intersection in mathematics and science

ROBERT M. MAY

Introduction

In putting together the programme for the 2011 Darwin Lectures with their theme of Beauty, the organisers aimed to begin with a lecture on Beauty and Mathematics. I believe it would indeed be possible to produce a riveting lecture or chapter strictly confined to this topic, narrowly construed. I have, however, taken the liberty of widening the discussion, to ask about the part played by considerations of elegance and aesthetics – by *beauty* – in humanity's age-old quest for understanding how the world works.

This being said, the chapter nevertheless begins with a discussion of what I hope is a persuasive account of the interplay between Beauty and Truth in purely mathematical contexts. Against this background, I go on to consider the extent to which Beauty has guided, and still does guide, our advances towards understanding how the real world actually works. The chapter concludes with a brief look at the more complex landscape of intersections among beliefs and values, beauty, truth and tomorrow's world.

Beauty and mathematics

The attribute that primarily distinguishes *Homo sapiens* from the wonderful diversity of other creatures we share our planet with is our self-conscious quest to comprehend the world around us and our place in it. The first stirrings of this search are lost in mists of magic and mysticism, whose beautiful but enigmatic traces remain in the caves at Altamira, in stone circles, and in other such reminders. In so far as these initial explorations had a 'scientific' component, it was observational and descriptive: movements of the stars and seasons; the behaviour of other animals; the nutritional and medicinal properties of plants. From these early investigations and philosophical speculations, the foundations of mathematical studies emerged and, unlike most other areas, survived essentially unchanged to the present. Here one starts with a set of defined axioms or propositions and then deduces the consequences within a closed logical system: if two sides of a Euclidian triangle are equal then two angles are equal; no 'ifs or buts'. Of course, such mathematical truths include a wider class of logical exercises, puzzles and paradoxes.

For generations of schoolchildren Euclidian geometry could indeed be the canonical example of mathematical truths, with individual students finding the proofs difficult or surprising or even enthrallingly beautiful. In all cases, *quod erat demonstrandum* means just what it says.

Given the right perspective, which too often will depend on one's early teachers, the 'truths' of mathematics are undoubtedly beautiful. Even so, such beauty is perhaps too cold, too icy for some. What follows is an attempt to share my perceptions of this beauty, with some examples.

Figure 1.1 illustrates one of the first theorems in Euclid's classic geometry text. It illustrates his proof, mentioned above, that if the triangle ABC has two sides equal (AB = AC), then two angles (at B and C) are equal. Euclid's proof consists of adding a line from A to intersect the line BC at right angles at D. Now the two triangles ABD and ACD are congruent (AB = AC; AD is common to both; the angles at D are the same, 90°, for both triangles). Therefore the angles at B and C are equal. QED.

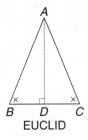

EUCLID

FIGURE 1.1. Euclid's theorem about isosceles triangles.

As a twelve-year-old, when I first encountered this theorem in my first year of secondary school, I argued with the teacher that the result was obvious, by symmetry. I was told, in no uncertain terms, that such intuitive arguments were not what geometry was about. One needed rigorous, formal proofs. I was therefore delighted with the following truly *beautiful* result.

In the 1950s, with the advent of the first computers, one creative group working on Artificial Intelligence (AI) decided that a good test of their computer's ability to think creatively would be to ask it to provide proofs of Euclid's theorems. And the above theorem seemed like a perfect example, because it would require from the computer the creative act of constructing the perpendicular line AD. But that is not what this genuinely creative computer did! It provided a rigorous version of the intuitively obvious symmetry argument. Consider the 'two triangles' ABC and ACB: the first triangle's side AB is equal to the second triangle's side AC (by definition); likewise the second sides AC = AB; and BC is common to both. Therefore the two triangles are congruent, and the angle B equals the angle C. No clumsy construction of a perpendicular is necessary! I find this proof, resonating over two millennia, truly beautiful.

Some very simple things in mathematics took some time to be recognized. It is not clear when humans first learned to count systematically beyond 1, 2, 3, ... Certainly early ways of encoding such counting were mostly clumsy (I, II, III, IV, ...). The early civilizations of Mesopotamia gave us a counting system essentially with a base of 60. This heritage persists in how we measure time and angles (60 does have the virtue of factoring in many ways). It was the Arabic world that gave us the numerals we use today, and − more fundamentally − the non-trivial concept of zero, 0. (This concept seems not to have arrived at demotic levels in the USA, where the ground or zeroth floor of buildings is called the 'first floor'). And the concept of negative numbers was even slower in arriving.

Less trivial, although hugely useful and important, is the concept of 'imaginary numbers'. Consider the simple quadratic equation

$$x^2 + 2x + 2 = 0. \qquad (1)$$

We can rewrite this as

$$(x + 1)^2 = -1,$$ (2)

which has the solution

$$x = -1 \pm \sqrt{-1}.$$ (3)

Wait a minute! Square root of -1! You cannot have a sensible number which, when multiplied by itself, gives you -1. But we can DEFINE the imaginary number i to be

$$i = \sqrt{-1}.$$ (4)

Now we can write the solutions of the quadratic equation (1) as

$$x = -1 \pm i.$$ (5)

This concept of imaginary numbers opens to us a two-dimensional world. The familiar 'real' numbers, both positive and negative, can be thought of as all lying along a line. But we now have a two-dimensional 'complex plane' in which purely imaginary numbers lie along a vertical line, ordinary numbers along a horizontal line, and more generally complex numbers anywhere. This is illustrated in Figure 1.2.

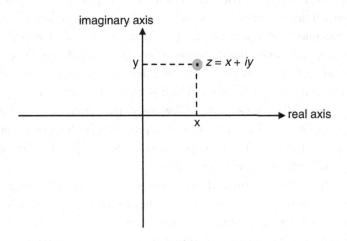

FIGURE 1.2. This figure illustrates the two-dimensional 'complex plane'. The horizontal axis represents real numbers, x, and the vertical axis imaginary numbers, y. A complex number, $z = x + iy$, is as shown.

Such complex numbers can alternatively be specified not by their distances along the real and imaginary axes, but equivalently by their distance from the origin (0, 0) and the angle they make with the horizontal axis. And this leads, *inter alia*, to one of the most magical equations I know (I have spared you the detailed proof):

$$e^{i\pi} = -1. \tag{6}$$

Here π is the ratio of the circumference of a circle to its diameter ($\pi = 3.1416...$), and e is a fundamental constant associated with the mathematical function, $f(x)$, possessing the property that, for all values of x, it has a rate of increase equal to $f(x)$. That is, e emerges from the solution of the differential equation $df/dx = f$, which is $f(x) = f(0)e^x$, where $e = 2.7182...$.

Equation (6) is truly astonishing. It connects two fundamental constants, π and e, which have concrete numerical values associated with the 'real world', and i, the basis for imaginary numbers. Alchemy pales by comparison!

If you think this equation (6) is a bit weird, wait till you see equation (7) and its properties:

$$x(t+1) = ax(t)[1 - x(t)]. \tag{7}$$

This equation has been proposed in several ecological contexts (fisheries, pest control and others), as a deliberately oversimplified description of the dynamical behaviour of the abundance of a population, $x(t)$, which has discrete, non-overlapping generations. The population in the next generation, $x(t + 1)$, depends on an intrinsic propensity to increase, proportional to some constant a, which is diminished by a feedback factor $[1 - x(t)]$ as $x(t)$ becomes larger. Obviously, the population will decline towards 0 if $a < 1$. Conversely, if x approaches its 'carrying capacity' (arbitrarily set at $x = 1$), the population in the next generation will be smaller (and extinct if x ever exceeds 1).

The extraordinary range of behaviour exhibited by this very simple equation is illustrated in Figure 1.3. If a lies in the range from 1 to 3, the population settles to a steady, stable value $x^* = (a - 1)/a$. This is exemplified by the lowest trajectory in Figure 1.3. Once a increases beyond 3, the population settles to regular up–down cycles of relative boom and bust, as exemplified by the central trajectory in Figure 1.3.

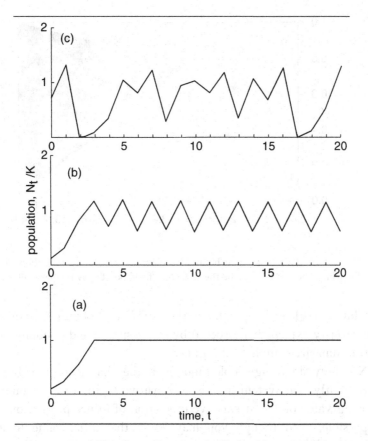

FIGURE 1.3. This figure illustrates the kinds of dynamical behaviour that the simple equation (7) can exhibit as the parameter a increases: (a) the system converges to a stable point; (b) stable two-point (up/down) cycles; (c) apparently random, or 'chaotic', behaviour.

These regular 'two-point' cycles then further bifurcate to give stable cycles of period 4, 8, 16, ... as a increases further. Once $a > 3.56$ ..., we enter a regime of what is now called 'chaos'. For all the world, the population looks as if it were fluctuating randomly, buffeted by environmental fluctuations. But in reality, the simple and purely deterministic model given in equation (7), with no random elements whatsoever in it, is giving this illusion of randomness, as illustrated by the top trajectory in Figure 1.3. Figure 1.4 illustrates the so-called 'bifurcation diagram' for this equation, showing how, as a increases from left to right, the system

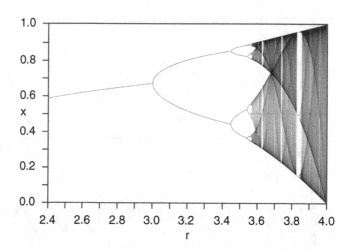

FIGURE 1.4. The 'bifurcation diagram' for equation (7), showing values of x for which the 'next x' will be the same (i.e. 'fixed points') as the parameter a varies.

exhibits a single stable point, and then stable two-point cycles of increasing severity, which then proceed by successive period doublings into an extraordinarily complicated regime.

Not only do things look random in the chaotic region, but, more importantly, the system here is so sensitive to the exact details of the starting value of x that effective prediction of future population sizes is impossible, even though you may know the initial value to a good approximation, and you have an equation with absolutely nothing random within it. Figure 1.5 illustrates this: the solid lines show the trajectory for the above equation, with $a = 3.8$ and the initial value of x being 0.300 (the solid lines) or alternatively 0.301 (the dashed lines). It will be seen that for the first few iterates the tiny difference between these two starting conditions makes little difference, but by the time one is ten time steps away from the beginning, the resulting population projections are about as different as they could be.

This is not some arcane mathematical curiosity. In a wider sense, it represents the end of the Newtonian dream. When I was a graduate student it was thought that prediction of local weather would simply get better and better, and reach further and further ahead, as computing power increased. But we now realize that the Navier–Stokes

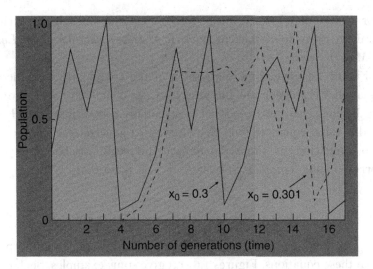

FIGURE 1.5. This figure shows how trajectories generated by the simple equation (7) depend extraordinarily sensitively on the starting value, $x(0)$, in the 'chaotic' region (here, $a = 3.8$). The solid lines correspond to starting with $x = 0.300$, and the dashed lines to starting with $x = 0.301$.

equations, which are fundamental to predictions about the weather, behave in a chaotic way. This means that the problem with longer-term local weather prediction – beyond the next twenty days or so – is not simply a matter of ever more refined measurement of the initial conditions, but rather that sensitivity to the tiniest effects in those initial conditions make it effectively impossible to predict beyond a relatively close time horizon. I should add that the models used on the larger questions of climate change are rather more robust, so that although we can predict long-term effects in global climate, for local weather the situation will always be as summarized in Tom Stoppard's play *Arcadia*:

> we're better at predicting events at the edge of the galaxy or inside
> the nucleus of an atom than whether it'll rain on auntie's garden party
> three Sundays from now … we can't even predict the next drip from a
> dripping tap when it gets irregular. Each drip sets up the conditions
> for the next, the smallest variation blows prediction apart, and the
> weather is unpredictable in the same way, will always be unpredictable.
> (Act 1, Scene 4)

For a more detailed account of these issues, see the relevant chapter in Graham Farmelo's excellent book *It Must be Beautiful: Great Equations of Modern Science.*[1]

Figure 1.4 gave some impression of the complexity that the simple equation (7) can generate. But vastly greater complexity, and accompanying Beauty, emerges from what is essentially a two-dimensional version of this same equation. One elegant way to generalize equation (7) into two dimensions is simply to replace the 'real' variable x in (7) by a corresponding 'complex' variable, $z = x + iy$, so that

$$x_{next} = a[x(1-x) + y^2],\tag{8a}$$

$$y_{next} = ay(1 - 2x).\tag{8b}$$

We can now generate gorgeously, almost mystically, beautiful patterns from these equations. Figures 1.6–1.9 give some examples. Such patterns are generated by first specifying the parameter a (which itself can be a complex number, although I simplified equations (8a, b) by taking a as real), and then plotting all the equation's 'fixed points' in the complex plane. That is, find all those points for which this 'complex quadratic' map does not diverge (i.e. $z_{next} = z$), remembering that these do not have to be stable fixed points.

In essence, this process is the two-dimensional analogue of taking the bifurcation diagram for the one-dimensional equation, Figure 1.4, and finding all the fixed points for a specified value of a in the messy, chaotic right-hand part of the figure.

In general, these beautiful patterns are called Julia Sets, after the French mathematician Gaston Julia, who discovered them in 1915. They were, however, brought centre stage by Benoît Mandelbrot, who rediscovered them around 1980, when computers were available fully to create such patterns. Figure 1.6 outlines the specific case of the Mandelbrot Set, with Figure 1.7 indicating more detail. One central feature of these sets is that you see more and more detail as you look on finer and finer scales. Figure 1.8 is such an expansion of detail from one 'twiddle' of Figure 1.6, and Figure 1.9 is a corresponding expansion of a detail from Figure 1.8.

---

[1] Graham Farmelo (ed.), *It Must be Beautiful: Great Equations of Modern Science* (London: Granta, 2002).

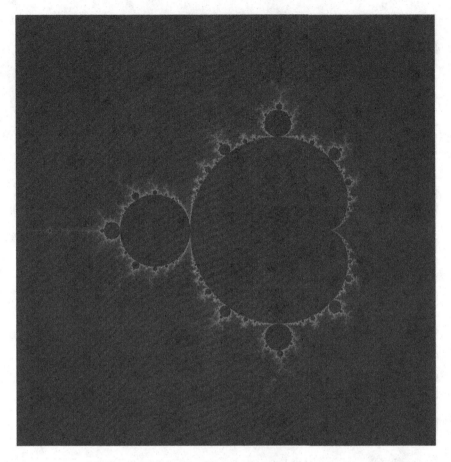

FIGURE 1.6. The interesting figure generated by the Mandelbrot Set (for details, see the text). Image produced by Philip Dawid using the program WinCIG Chaos Image Generator developed by Thomas Hövel.

Another notably peculiar feature of such two-dimensional patterns is illustrated specifically by Figure 1.6 for the Mandelbrot Set. In Figure 1.6 the entire set, as illustrated, lies within a circle of radius 2.5 centred on (0, 0) in the complex plane. So the area bounded by the twiddly red line is explicitly finite. But the length of this twiddly boundary itself is infinite! This can alternatively be expressed by saying that this seemingly one-dimensional boundary actually has a 'fractal dimension' of 2.

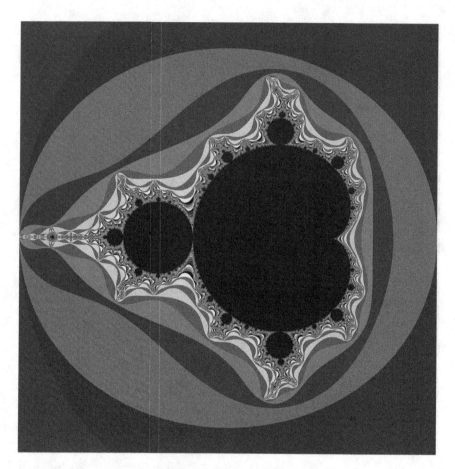

FIGURE 1.7. The same Mandelbrot Set, but with the fine details (which reach beyond the red boundary shown in Figure 1.6 in tiny filaments which are virtually invisible) indicated by colouring regions in which they can be found (yellow to green to shades of red as the tendrils get ever wispier). For colour images, see www.darwin.cam. ac.uk/lectures/beauty. Image produced by Philip Dawid using the program WinCIG Chaos Image Generator developed by Thomas Hövel.

I end this section on Beauty and Mathematics with a caveat. Not all of mathematics is about apodictic truths. For one thing, we can often be fairly sure a theorem is true, but unable to prove it. Over a century ago, David Hilbert famously set out a list of important but unsolved mathematical problems. The Clay Foundation marked the turn of the millennium by announcing million-dollar prizes for proofs of the seven still-unsolved

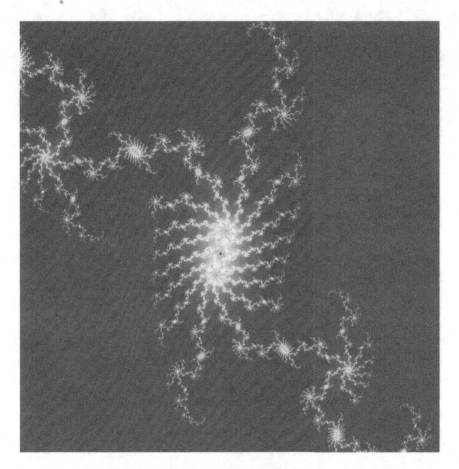

FIGURE 1.8. One of the tendrils from the boundary shown in Figure 1.6, but much enlarged, so that intricate details can be seen. Image produced by Philip Dawid using the program WinCIG Chaos Image Generator developed by Thomas Hövel.

Hilbert problems. Some of these problems, moreover, have important practical applications: a solution to the Riemann Hypothesis, for example, could have serious implications for widely used methods of encrypting information. Fermat's 'last theorem' resisted proof for centuries.

Particularly interesting is the 'four-colour problem', which conjectures that no more than four colours are needed unambiguously to distinguish the territories in any conceivable map. Having frustrated mathematicians for centuries, this theorem was relatively recently proved by a computer program which explored a vast number of categories of 'exceptional cases',

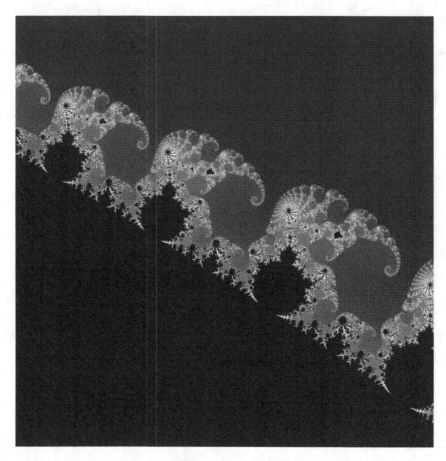

FIGURE 1.9. A yet further expansion, to show a 'procession of elephants(!)', hidden in one of the tendrils of Figure 1.8. Ever more detail can be seen on endlessly finer scales. This, incidentally, is the essence of fractal geometry. Image produced by Philip Dawid using the program WinCIG Chaos Image Generator developed by Thomas Hövel.

thus eliminating all possible counter-examples. Many felt that such an ugly proof, which provides essentially no deeper insight into this mathematical problem, is undeserving of the appellation 'proof'. A similarly brute-force computer proof has very recently shown that, as long surmised, the game of draughts or chequers is a draw with best play on both sides. One day we may even have a similar proof for chess (for which the question is, in principle, clear), but here the corresponding computation is so huge that any such result lies in the far, far distant future.

A more radical issue was raised by Gödel's theorem, which shows that some kinds of mathematical questions are simply undecidable. The 'class of all classes not members of a given class' is perhaps the simplest example, although some would prefer to sequester such problems, re-labelling them as paradoxes.

Beauty and the natural sciences

Beauty is truth,
truth beauty – that is all
Ye know on earth
and all ye need to know.

Keats, 1819

Mathematics underpins much of the natural sciences. This is transparently true in the physical sciences, and increasingly recognized in important aspects of the life sciences, ranging from ecology and evolution to gene sequencing. One interesting but extreme view was enunciated by Galileo, describing the universe: 'This grand book is written in the language of mathematics, and its characters are triangles, circles and other geometric objects.' This is still true of much of physics. It guides quite a few string theorists and other seekers of a Grand Unified Theory, subject to the recognition that the language of mathematics is vastly richer than triangles, circles and other geometric objects, but rather has to embrace fractal geometries and deterministic chaos.

But the nature of the quest in the natural sciences differs somewhat from that in mathematics, in that one is not working with closed logical systems, but rather trying to understand, by a combination of observation, theory and experiment, the working of the world around us.

Both archaeological and anthropological evidence suggest that in its early days this quest involved a blend of what might be called scientific truths and beliefs/values: description and observation, yes; but also constrained by revelation and authority.

Going beyond description and observation, real progress in understanding how the natural world works only truly began with the Enlightenment, with its guiding principle that the truth is to be found not by appeal to authority but by experimental tests and evidence. This being acknowledged, and also recognizing that all such 'truths' are to a greater or lesser degree contingent on subsequent discoveries, the question of whether Beauty can be a useful guide to scientific truths remains interesting.

My personal view is that Keats, allowing for poetic licence, had a point. But the overriding precept for Truth in science is that an ugly fact trumps a beautiful theory. That being admitted, it remains remarkably true that Beauty can be and has been, on occasion, spectacularly successful. Two illustrative examples follow.

Einstein's Theory of Special Relativity is a prime example where considerations of elegance and Beauty, prompted by the utterly mystifying results of an important experiment, helped shape a truly revolutionary change in how we think about space, time and energy.

In the middle 1800s James Clerk Maxwell built on earlier experimental work to show how electrical and magnetic fields (which at that time were thought of as separate phenomena) could be elegantly unified within a common framework. This led to the concept of a pervasive 'ether', within which such fields were propagated. In turn, this motivated Michelson and Morley to design an ingenious experiment to measure our planet's motion relative to this ether. The results, in 1887, were very puzzling. They seemed to imply that the speed of light, c, as seen by any observer, was an absolute, unvarying constant, the same for all observers regardless of their relative movements. This, of course, was flatly inconsistent with classical Newtonian physics.

Stepping outside the Newtonian world, Einstein first observed that the fact that the value of c was independent of the observer's relative motion, coupled with the assumption that the laws of physics were the same at all times and all places, implied that measurements of time and space were *not* absolute, differing from one observer to another depending on their relative movements. This completely defies everyday intuition, which of course has no experience with speeds approaching that of light.

These assumptions then led Einstein to formulate equations describing, as it were, the behaviour of the clocks and yardsticks of an observer moving with velocity v in a four-dimensional space–time continuum (three spatial dimensions and time). One major implication of this fundamental change of perspective is a redefinition of the momentum, p, of an object of mass m moving at velocity v relative to an observer: the classical $p = mv$ is replaced by $p = \gamma mv$, where $\gamma = 1/(1 - v^2/c^2)^{1/2}$.

This symmetrical treatment of space and time is not only mathematically beautiful, but it has a further surprising implication, of great consequence. Whilst the three spatial dimensions are associated with momentum, which in turn generates the kinetic energy associated with a moving mass, the analogous association of time in Einstein's Beauty-prompted analysis is with the 'rest energy', $m_0 = mc^2$, of a body with mass m. This heretofore unexpected rest energy has the further astonishing implication that if mass can – in a fundamental sense – be lost, then that lost mass's rest energy must appear in some other form. Ever since the first mushroom cloud blossomed in the deserts of Nevada, we fully appreciate how such mass can be lost in nuclear fission, and how devastating the 'other forms' of the lost rest mass can be.

In everyday life these differences between the physics of Special Relativity and classical Newtonian physics essentially never show up, because v is vastly smaller than c. This can be seen explicitly and elegantly, by looking at Einstein's definition of the energy of a body of mass m moving at velocity v:

$$E^2 = m^2 c^4 + p^2 c^2 \tag{9}$$

Here, as above, $p = \gamma mv$ and the energy associated with the three spatial dimensions is pc; the corresponding energy associated with the time dimension is mc^2. We can thus rewrite equation (9) as $E^2 = \gamma^2 m^2 c^4 (\gamma^{-2} + v^2/c^2)$, which simplifies to

$$E = mc^2/(1 - v^2/c^2)^{1/2} \tag{10}$$

In the limit of $v \ll c$, as corresponds to everyday experience, we can approximate equation (10) as

$$E = (mc^2) + \frac{1}{2}mv^2. \tag{11}$$

The mc^2 term, corresponding to Einstein's 'rest energy', of course appears nowhere in classical physics. The second term is the Newtonian kinetic energy, familiar to all schoolchildren. Omitted are correction terms of relative order v^2/c^2, and thus usually negligible.

Robert M. May

All in all, Einstein's fusion of Michelson–Morley's puzzling fact with hugely imaginative mathematical elegance on the one hand resonates with Keats's poem, whilst on the other has vastly important practical implications.

Perhaps even more amazing as an example of Beauty turning the conventional world of science upside down is the Dirac Equation and its seemingly ridiculous implications.

In 1928 Paul Dirac set out to reformulate quantum mechanics, essentially as expressed by the Schrödinger Equation, in a form consistent with Special Relativity. In what follows I aim to sketch the gist of how he went about this, and of the new vistas it opened up, without getting into the technical details. Those wishing to go further should consult Graham Farmelo's superb biography of Dirac, *The Strangest Man*.[2]

The actual equation can be written in several different ways, but I choose the version inscribed on his memorial in Westminster Abbey:

$$i\gamma.\delta\psi = m\psi. \tag{12}$$

Here we really have four equations, because the symbol γ stands for a 4×4 matrix, and the related symbol δ stands for a vector operator which differentiates with respect to the 4 space–time variables x, y, z, t. The function $\psi(x, y, z, t)$ is a 'wave function', akin to that introduced by Schrödinger in his equation: ψ gives a probabilistic description of the state of the system in space and time. Various physical constants have been eliminated by rescaling, and i is our imaginary friend from equation (4).

Dirac's equation is logical in its construction, gorgeous in its simplicity, but astounding in its implications. The 4×4 matrix γ corresponds to the four dimensions of space–time, and to four distinct states which represent particles. Two of these states/particles are familiar: electrons with their negative charge and positive rest energy, along with spin either up or down. The other two states similarly correspond to spin up or down, but now for elementary particles with negative rest energy. What are these enigmatic particles? Dirac initially hoped these might turn out to be protons. But protons have a much larger mass than electrons (roughly 1,836 times), which is essentially impossible to

---

[2] Graham Farmelo, *The Strangest Man: The Hidden Life of Paul Dirac, Quantum Genius* (London: Faber & Faber, 2009).

reconcile with symmetries implicit in the equation. A further problem is that these two particles must have negative rest energy.

So Dirac then made an astoundingly imaginative leap: these states/particles must be anti-electrons. But there is still a problem. Given that radiative transitions are possible from a state of positive energy to one of negative energy, why do we not commonly observe electrons making such transitions? Dirac now went further to suggest that the normal, though as yet unrecognized, state of the universe is that essentially all such 'negative-energy electron' states are full. Assuming that there are no electromagnetic or gravitational effects of these anti-electrons, we will only notice them when deviations from the norm, produced by emptying one or more of the negative energy states, are observed. That is, given these radical assumptions, this hidden and essentially fully occupied world of negatively charged electrons with negative energy could only manifest itself by the occasional absence of such a negative charge/negative mass particle, which 'hole' (in the cosmic background) would show up as a positively charged particle with similarly positive rest mass and kinetic energy. Hence, the 'hole' theory of 'positrons'.

I believe this is *the* most extreme example of a scientific theory based on symmetry, elegance and sheer beauty, not to mention mind-blowing assumptions about the not-yet-seen. But it was quickly shown to provide a very accurate estimate of the magnetic moment of an electron, and to explain – to high accuracy – the detailed 'fine structure' of atomic spectral lines.

And to clinch it, in 1932 experiments detected positrons, with properties as predicted. Dirac received the Nobel Prize for physics the next year. As an example of creativity guided by Beauty, I think Dirac's Equation beats even Einstein's Relativity. I find it odd that the latter is so widely recognized and the former not. Admittedly Dirac shunned publicity, and Einstein courted it, but that seems an insufficient explanation.

Against the above two examples of Beauty and scientific truths walking hand-in-hand, most of modern science is much less spectacular. I believe physics continues to give the best examples, largely because fundamental laws, such as conservation of energy and momentum, along with other conservation rules, underpin so much. Certainly some of the wilder frontiers of string theory exemplify mathematical elegance coupled with very bold speculation, although it remains to be seen whether triumphs to parallel Einstein and Dirac will result.

The life sciences are typically messier. Although the same basic physics ultimately underlies everything we see, the complexities that evolutionary processes have produced in varying environments over eons of time make the subject less susceptible to basic and beautiful simplicities. By way of compensation, these same processes give us the natural beauty, of plants, animals and landscapes, that will receive attention elsewhere in this book. And the social sciences have all the problems of complications found in the life sciences, further compounded by the subjects' being affected by observation and policy choices. This also is a subject explored extensively in later chapters, but I now touch on it in my short concluding section.

Beliefs and values: truth, beauty and tomorrow's world

There are, of course, important questions about objective truth and about beauty which – while they eventually may make contact with our growing understanding of neurobiology and the evolution of behaviour of individuals and communities – lie largely outside the domain of today's science. Some such questions are: what is happiness?; how do we handle the trade-offs between the rights of individuals and the collective interests of society (e.g. the arguments for and against compulsory childhood vaccination or identity cards)?; and ultimately, what is the meaning of life?

For many, answers to essentially all such questions are ultimately provided by one or other of the world's religions, monotheistic or otherwise. Here the canonical texts set out the basic principles which have, in effect, usually been interpreted, elaborated, and quite often twisted out of shape by successive generations of learned teachers and scholars. Other belief systems, based for example on the writings of Marx or Mao, although disclaiming any religious connection, have served a similar purpose over the past century and more.

More generally, although the Enlightenment is characterized by its espousal of liberty of individual conscience and rejection of the authoritarian certitudes of dogma or revelation, the values it endorses build on the best of what went before. My personal belief is that most of the world's population either do, or would if they were allowed, embrace the beautifully expressed values enshrined in the American Constitution: life, liberty, and the pursuit of happiness. These are also implicit in the United Nations Charter, and more recently in its Millennium Development Goals.

However, in a finite world under increasing pressure from too many people with consequent difficulties for supplies of food and water, for the survival of other species, and all compounded by climate change, there are inherent conflicts between actions that we need to take collectively and the costs to individuals that these imply. This leads us to the central truth of our time, namely that we need better understanding of the evolution of cooperative behaviour, along with better understanding of the resulting origins and dynamics of our institutional structures, and ultimately better understanding at the interface between scientific truths and beliefs/values.

As humanity collectively makes its choices about tomorrow's world, the job of science is to frame the debate clearly, making plain the likely benefits and costs of these choices – and the concomitant uncertainties. And making clear that cloud-cuckoo-land is not a feasible choice. When it comes to acting out the demographic drama of choice on the stage thus set, my hope would be that Beauty and Truth come together in our decisions about what kind of world we want.

2 Beauty and the grotesque

JOSÉ HERNÁNDEZ

I find myself in something of a quandary, not only because of the essential differences between the Spanish and English languages but also because writing is not, and never has been, the natural mode of expression for a painter, and I am no exception to the rule. My translator, moreover, has had to cope with my personal linguistic quirks, perhaps a trifle baroque, and this has been a further source of complication. You are, therefore, regretfully forewarned. I shall do everything in my power to convey to you as accurately as possible my feelings, rather than ideas, concerning 'beauty and the grotesque'.

Despite all the obstacles, and believing as I do that what really counts is communication, whether by means of words or signs, I think that the best thing I can do, to start with, is to tell you something of my personal experience as an artist: that is to say, of the insatiable curiosity that has driven me all my life to try my hand, albeit timidly, at other disciplines. These disciplines have turned out to be complementary to my principal activity as a painter: engraving, the illustration of literary texts, the production of sets for theatre, and sculpture. To conclude this preamble, I must insist that I am not writing as a specialist in beauty, aesthetics or semiotics. To pose as such would be to indulge in impersonation, hypocrisy and pedantry, all of which vices I detest. As for my views on the 'ugly' or 'the grotesque', I hope that they will become clear later in my comments on their paradoxical relation to beauty.

Let me explain first, then, that I was born to paint, and began quite spontaneously before I reached my adolescence, in a setting completely alien to such an activity and in circumstances hardly propitious, one would have thought, to artistic inclinations. The scarce knowledge of art that I possess was acquired in the first place through the practice of

26

painting itself and, later, through reading – all of this with no other purpose than to become a person, to find my way in the world. My dreams gave rise to more dreams. Some of them, lots of them, began to materialize, so much so that I am still part of them. For example, I draw and paint every single day of my life. In those early flights of imagination I proved – or, better, I discovered – that beauty existed not only in nature but also in paintings, words, sounds and gestures and so on. Little by little my naivety began to turn into something more real, something more difficult to cope with: I refer to ignorance. Some day it had to happen – and it did. I realized that painting and creativity were more than simply that; that painting, in itself, was almost of secondary importance; that one had to go deeper. I grasped that the mere contemplation that I had practised up to then was tantamount to remaining satisfied with the surface of things. I perceived that things were no longer simply 'pretty': that some of them, moreover, were beautiful. From those dreams, among those dreams, I learnt 'in a blink of an eye' ('in ictu oculi') to compare these dreams with the external world. I learnt to distinguish in the midst of diversity, to give things their names and to weigh them up (with the corresponding risk this involved). I learnt what beauty meant for me and for others. I admit that this made me feel different and that I suffered without understanding what this new phenomenon signified for me at a personal level. It took me a while to comprehend what the prodigy of beauty signified in the aesthetic category, such as in Greek art. I grasped that, despite the diversity of tastes, tendencies or circumstances, artists succeeded in stamping their own style on their works, giving us certain clues to a better understanding of their respective personalities and, with this, their different visions or interpretations of beauty.

There are innumerable versions of the same image or theme that, for diverse reasons, have become icons. And this makes us think that terms or concepts such as beauty can vary or be interpreted in very different ways without losing their essence. In any event, one cannot believe before starting out to paint that one is in the process of creating beauty because, no matter how exact the formula, if there be such, it is the *result* that proves whether a work attains the category of the beautiful. Beauty, that is, cannot be fabricated at will. The aesthetic object only manifests itself, or fails to do so, in the external world once the imagined work has come into existence.

One theory of the origin of art holds that the empirical reality mixes the beautiful and the ugly automatically, just as nature does, so that in order to enjoy the beautiful in itself and for itself, it must have been produced or included in a familiar context. As a theory it is valid enough, although somewhat restrictive nowadays since the familiar context can be different or, generalizing, its point of departure can be fiction. Frankly, I am not sure about this or other theories, since in my case the impulse to begin a painting comes directly from a sensation captured or visualized, relatively quickly, on paper, most frequently without allowing any disturbance or attention to the so-called rules to inhibit or delay the representation of the initial prompting. In fact no premeditation is involved – or very little, since the process is more spontaneous than otherwise. Later there may be changes, but these are generally minimal. Another phenomenon, which normally occurs at the fearful moment in which one has to face the as yet immaculate surface of the canvas or drawing paper, is a sensation of vertigo, a vertigo that lasts as long as the sensation itself, whether this be protracted or ephemeral.

Well, going back to my beginnings, the die was cast: I had to be a painter before all else – that was clear. And I needed to know, urgently, the answer to a pressing question: If it was art that brought beauty to our attention, what brought the ugly? And if it was beauty, what, then, was ugliness? Was it the opposite, with the same consistency, the same meaning, but in the opposite sense? More questions came to me one after another. I found that reading was the only process that helped me to situate these values at points where I could grasp their significance. I went on painting, of course, painting naturally, almost in a frenzy, as I still do, reaching out for everything that presented itself without knowing whether it was good or bad – including for the health of the adolescent I was then.

My conclusions – or, rather, revelations – allowed me to continue my way along the mysterious path, avid to discover how to become myself, no matter what happened afterwards, avid to launch out into territory, if as yet unknown, *intuited*. I still ask myself, to tell the truth, how I came to feel, to sense, the nearness of beauty before knowing that such a thing existed and had a name.

Diego de Velázquez's painting *Venus at her Mirror* represents for an artist one of the clearest examples of beauty in painting. Evidently there

FIGURE 2.1. This picture could represent any little corner in any studio and of any artist/painter. In this case it is my habitat, where I live, the space where I let myself be surprised every day and where my dreams, when I am lucky, become a sketch. Image appears by courtesy of the artist.

are other examples by other authors, but of this one in particular, with the objectivity that is required, one could confidently assert that, besides the genius of the painter, it represents the balance and the proper measure in the use of its components. It deals with, in the end, a perfect work of art in the formal sense of the term. Putting to one side, for the moment, other considerations, such as what might happen to me, the mere intention became what I most yearned for: knowledge of something called 'beauty' and its affinities. I set out, as bravely as possible, on my search – for and initiated by my 'artistic adventure' – convinced that it was my destiny. It was an uncertain destiny, to be sure, but one that I felt intuitively would bring me something uniquely different, something inspiring, something that I was looking for and not finding in my current environment. Clearly my vital interests were now of another order.

Painting was no longer merely a representation of what I saw around me but something invisible that urged me to explore imaginary territories. It was not always necessary, either, to transfer these diffuse imaginings onto paper. To feel satisfied, it was enough to have experienced having imagined them, or, at most, simply to make a few jottings in a notebook.

The experience could hardly have been more arresting – or, better, fascinating. The jottings were equivalent to the numerous drawings heaped on my desk or pinned to the wall, drawings that later, perhaps, would be turned, or not, into paintings and engravings. There were no guarantees, but I have to say that such a system enabled me, and still does, to live my reveries more intensely and pleasurably. The construction of a personal set of values was becoming as essential to me as was the acquisition of certain technical rudiments.

Meanwhile I never stopped asking myself if ugliness was really the opposite of beauty. And, if this were so, what place was occupied by the grotesque? We know that another source of attraction is ugliness. If it is true that the equations ugly equals bad and beauty equals good exist, then we will not be surprised to learn that the one is as ancient as the other and that both were born simultaneously, with the resulting and inevitable doubt concerning preference for one or the other. More than *when*, I was concerned to know *which* were the first criteria used to define the terms beauty, the ugly, the grotesque, the sinister. The idea of the shadow was particularly poignant for me: What does the love of shadows suggest to us? Shadows have always been more related to the sinister than to beauty, yet there is a paradox here because a shadow can also be beautiful, as beautiful as light. As can be seen, our habitual codes are of little use in cases such as these, in which the senses and instinct lead us to what gives us pleasure, relief, well-being. Does it emerge, then, that the primitive and instinctual notion of good and evil is not so crazy after all? To pose and answer these questions, to uncover the unknown, to come close to the threshold of mystery is what enriches and permits us to acquire a certain ability to reason, to discern, to choose what is most suited to our needs, and to avoid what makes us experience fear, unease, rejection or repugnance. This is all very well indeed, although I may disagree at times: What about the other pleasure, the pleasure produced by transgression, which is itself the process of a metamorphosis and the

FIGURE 2.2. This image could illustrate a long discourse about the tremendous power of the imagination. The strength with which this title is expressed says much of the author's personality and his resistance to making concessions. Diego Velazquez, *The Toilet of Venus* © The National Gallery, London. Presented by The Art Fund, 1906.

potential for things to be otherwise? Let us not forget Goya's asseveration that 'the sleep of reason produces monsters'.

What are these feelings that move us to transgress, to infringe established precepts? Is it perhaps reason itself that enjoins us to do so? And is this not the grotesque?

To the grotesque are applied also other pejorative terms such as ridiculous, extravagant, capricious or irregular. This being so, we would have the same reaction on seeing a top hat, a moustache, a portrait, the funnel of a transatlantic steamer, a bulldog, a pig, and so on, or on perceiving the reverberation of a sound. But it is not so. Nothing that man has created can be alien to him and nobody can deny that these examples are also authentic creations like any other. (Allow me to disagree with appreciations that have more to do with certain moral prejudices than with aesthetic deductions.) Close to the grotesque we also find in currency terms such as the fantastic, the oneiric: spaces in

FIGURE 2.3. *El Pájaro de la Noche* (1986) by José Hernández. Image appears by courtesy of the artist.

which are represented the imagined creatures whose morphology does not always coincide with those of real life, spaces where often something indefinable undergoes distortion, where the mind is unable to control the impulses that only affect the person who dreams.

Now that we are imagining, let us remember that in the Hellenistic period, which has had such an influence on our Western culture, endeavours such as art, philosophy, literature and navigation led to the exploration of distant lands, thereby greatly broadening our knowledge of other civilizations, with their descriptions, mainly legendary and rich in fantasy, in which there appear misshapen human forms, monstrous animals, fauns, creatures with no heads, androgynies, chimaeras and so on and so forth. The encyclopaedias incorporated these never-previously-imagined figures in their pages, thereby greatly

FIGURE 2.4. *Dura el Tránsito* (1981) by José Hernández. Image appears by courtesy of the artist.

enlarging our general culture with a panoply of monsters that generate fear, monsters used as a threat against whoever fails to comply with the norms imposed by those in power.

Beauty, as I understand it, is a combination of at times indefinable elements which, ordered in a precise manner, make it possible for that which is represented in, for example, a painting, to exert an attraction that transcends forms, colours and textures. This reasoning is pretty basic, I know, but I believe it constitutes a valid departure point for an interesting debate, a debate that could enable us to know the opinions of creative artists and give rise to some surprising conclusions and comments concerning cognate expressions or synonyms for beauty. These include conceptions such as prettiness, the sublime, loveliness, excellence and the morbid. The last of these is associated pejoratively with other questions and is, in principle, unrelated to our main subject. We also find other less

FIGURE 2.5. This is a fragment, chosen at random, of the mural paintings of the Triclinium in Villa Carmiano on the theme of Neptune and Amymone in the first century AD, on the Varano Hill, Gulf of Naples. In my judgement the feminine figure is of extraordinary beauty in spite of having been extracted from a conjuncture which has been denominated GROTESQUE for purely formal reasons. Villa Carmiano Triclinio.

common manifestations of this tendency to define certain themes negatively in the variety of opinions expressed by certain observers, visitors to museums and even to artists' studios. These observers can arrive at curious, conflicting and even aberrant conclusions over the same matters, and these opinions often separate more than they approximate.

The persistence of the idea that sensitivity is a sign of weakness proves the necessity of constantly revising these values, and may necessitate an interrogation of the virtues of the education system of a society such as ours, a society little given to reflection and more inclined to banality and insane consumerism. I am among those who believe that nothing is exclusive, that everything is complementary. In this sense I believe in harmony in all its varieties and that this, too, is beauty. I am also convinced, generally, that despite the disequilibrium produced by exclusions, art is more necessary now than ever and that the better we succeed in expressing ourselves and communicating with others the greater the pleasure. With regard to education I must insist again that, in art, feeling is more important than mere dexterity. The extraordinary evolution of the technology to which we have access nowadays signifies, or should signify, that perfection is ever closer. Perfection in this case is art, and art is the shortest route, as I said before, to the achievement of non-exclusive values. For reasons of mental hygiene we should not be ashamed of expressing our feelings and should allow them to flow naturally. I must reiterate that such an attitude is not an indication of weakness but, rather, a virtue.

To advance in knowledge it is necessary to apportion names not only to objects but to effects, sensations and other manifestations of the human being and his spirit and to those of all-embracing nature. I recognize that, while not giving much importance to models, rules and other impositions, a certain familiarity with the art of painting has helped me to express my feeling and desires – in short, to live. I recognize equally that at times I have broken with certain conventions, something about which I am unrepentant. The work that I have managed to produce up to now will have to express itself. What I can say is that in creating it I have learned to be myself, which was my purpose from the beginning. I continue to make discoveries every day, my capacity for surprise is endless, my enthusiasm also. I search and sometimes I even find! The solitude of my studio welcomes and stimulates me. The accumulation of diverse objects that surround me disturbs me a bit, but they all form part of an atmosphere that it would be difficult for me to live without. They all contribute to a state of mind which encourages me to continue and that is what I do.

With regard to *atmosphere*, I must add that this is precisely the effect I seek to achieve in a picture, as it is the effect that enables me to recognize myself in it. The fact that we admit the canon of beauty as a regulating or guiding principle does not mean that it is not subject to different interpretations. What is beyond discussion is that it is a reality, a variable reality if you like, but a reality. This can be shown by its evolution through the years, gathering along the way, quite naturally, seemingly irreconcilable contradictions and paradoxes. But, I repeat, I believe that this is how it should be. For me, beauty has always had more to do with intuition than with respect for a canon that, moreover, has changed down the years in accordance with the usages, modes, or other needs depending on the moment and the place. By way of example it is interesting to note how certain Renaissance authors, much given to didactics, in this case Fine Arts didactics, hold forth in certain catalogues of iconography. In these catalogues we find extensive descriptions of beauty that show us a young woman bearing, as well as her own physical attributes, a series of symbolic objects that contribute singularly to exalt her figure. (This also occurs in catalogues of architecture.)

Again, what can be said regarding the tyranny of beauty and how a person can subject himself or herself to a physical pursuit that in our age normalizes plastic surgery, an operation known frequently as 'aesthetic'? What is the ideal pursued? Are we dealing with a desire for beauty comparable to that of the creative artist? I say no. I do not think that these developments have affected or modified the essence of the concept. I would say, rather, the opposite: that they have hugely broadened the spectrum, borrowing from the plastic arts one of their most striking antagonisms: the grotesque.

The grotesque, frequently considered – unjustly – a lesser art, was born practically at the same time as classicism in painting and ornamental sculpture. I still remember the impression, or rather, the shock to my system, the first time I saw, first in books and then in reality, a Romanesque façade or capital with terrifying sculpted scenes, supposedly of a moralizing influence, or the gargoyles that proliferate in our gloomy Gothic cathedrals. Are morality and exemplarity the best examples of beauty? Not exactly. Were they perhaps examples of the grotesque? At all events they were and are works that, stripped of their truculent messages, turn out to be artistically and objectively admirable although they do not belong to the category of the beautiful or of the ugly. And for that matter, what is the ugly? Is ugly the opposite of beautiful, perhaps, or that which does not fit in with the infallible formula of a given concept or precept? But let us return to what really interests us; we must continue to ask what beauty means to us personally. Beauty is what one imagines it to be; it is in the eye of the beholder. However, we must go beyond this celebrated aphorism.

It is said, and it seems likely, that the imagination knows no limits. If this is true, it could also be said that, if there were limits they would be those of the human being. Often imagination transforms into beauty what is not beautiful, and the reverse. Here is the crux of the matter. Idealization is often linked to people's imaginative capacities, and this can cause many surprises. Art is a human product and, as such, it speaks to human beings about themselves. Let us not forget the human capacity to imagine things that are invisible but can be perceived without giving any explication. In the literature and art of the fantastic, it is said, we are transported in imagination to unknown worlds where people like ourselves suddenly find themselves in the presence of the inexplicable. Only by means of such intimate perceptions do we really succeed in distinguishing between what we like and do not like, between what attracts and repels us, between what transmits to us a sort of positive energy or, on the contrary, what makes us miserable. Here we may draw closer to the definition of beauty; we may penetrate deeper, but, due to beauty's essential mystery, we are certain only of never arriving at the bottom of the question. As I promised earlier, I am only writing about my personal experience as a painter. Painting is my little oracle, my refuge, where I can hopefully shed light on these questions, these mysteries. When I am in luck, some of their secrets come to me in a sort of catharsis, a sort of permanent introspection searching desperately for a way out of the tunnel. In this respect, when I am asked why I am so attracted to themes that fall outside the normal run of things, I usually adopt a dramatic tone and say that I began to paint more out of despair than by vocation, that something impelled me to communicate with my fellow human beings by this means and no other. This is the reason that I have never stopped looking for the best, the optimum, for that which I want to imagine lies at one end of the tunnel.

Returning to beauty, we know that in almost all cultures the beautiful has always been related with the good, and the ugly with the bad. This does not mean that we must accept it as an infallible formula. In fact, it is a simplification that does not add anything to our understanding of the subject. Although I recognize that on occasions it has been, if not true, at least useful or helpful for those for whom these sorts of considerations have never been a priority, for those who have never felt the need to cultivate the sensibility that, more or less developed, exists in all human beings. Some will have been unaware that they possess this ability; others will have sought to deny it out of shame or for fear of appearing weak. What is certain is that these values help to shape our taste and, in consequence, what enables us to enjoy our preferences. They facilitate access not only to the works created by mankind but also to whatever object or telluric manifestation that can be perceived, or felt, as beautiful.

So far I have been talking about the significance that beauty has for me, and also its antagonist, the grotesque, which I locate somewhere between the beautiful and the ugly. But this is also inexact, and for this reason it is necessary, if not to establish fixed boundaries, then at least to explore the differences between beauty and the grotesque, which are – on some occasions – evident and irrefutable. Sometimes it is difficult to pinpoint these concepts satisfactorily, but they are not as ambiguous as is commonly thought. There are those who maintain the hypothesis that in the wide universe of the grotesque there is also room for beauty, although each of these concepts has its own peculiarities.

The conflict between beauty and the grotesque neither scandalizes nor disturbs me. On the contrary, for me it opens the door to the imagination lacking in so many works of art that are considered superior solely because they are beautiful. Even the most orthodox authorities must recognize or appreciate the beautiful elements contained in certain works that are deemed grotesque. These works may not be 'great art', but it is nonetheless true that these representations intervene in the conflict between beauty and the grotesque and place on equal terms what we could call 'good taste', exuberant imagination, and other geometrical or purely pictorial elements of the first order.

In general these basically decorative paintings, such as the Triclinium mural, contain a considerable amount of competent workmanship, skill and a remarkable technical ability. Taken as a whole, their discourse is more superficial, dispersed, and at times even insubstantial and apparently of little depth compared with those other works termed 'major'. Even so, the grotesque is an artistic category, perfectly defined, and is not a recent phenomenon. Indeed, the term derives from 'grotto' and can be considered as being born simultaneously with classicism. Since then it has passed from the merely ornamental to another status, almost as broad as any other style. The decorative panels of the Roman villas, as well as the architectural elements from the Romanesque, can be seen very much in the

FIGURE 2.6. This image reproduces one of my oil paintings entitled *The Anchored Dream*. It represents a constant theme in my work: the dream, the dreamed or the to be dreamed. It is this oneiric theme that according to the art critics constitutes the basis of my creativity. *El Sueno Anclado* (2004) by José Hernández. Image appears by courtesy of the artist.

same line as the – quite disturbing – bestiaries of those periods. Both of these have awakened my interest and have influenced my painting. If the search for beauty was important, these discoveries were nonetheless so. It would seem that all of this is what I needed in order to define my identity and to continue exploring those apparently opposed worlds. In my search and through the study of the Renaissance, above all in Italy, I found more peace of mind. I could extract aesthetic and technical benefits. Learning was decisive. Accompanied by these findings I added my interest in the Baroque, where beauty and the grotesque were melted down into something close to ugliness.

Along with this knowledge I was fascinated by other images, new images, from the eighteenth century, which referred me back, once again, to the grotesque, now with an added satirical sense. In order to shorten my narration, let us go to the end of the nineteenth century, and the beginning of the twentieth, a period when the grotesque, virulent criticism, the satirical and finally the art of protest became the order of the day. These works not only remain as criticism but have a place in the great history of universal art by dint of their outstanding, one might say indisputable, quality. We find the same thing in literature and in the theatre, from domestic comedies to rural dramas. It resurfaces in fashion and its striking and extravagant complements: those 'Archimboldesque' hats made of fruits, or with taxidermic jewels such as birds in a nest; the leopard-skin coats and tube-like skirts; from the design of a dragonfly lamp to a bridal gown constructed like a wedding cake, or the design of an exquisite funereal statuary. I have taken the liberty of saying, somewhat boldly, that in art nothing is exclusive, which does not mean, of course, that everything is valid. The practice of exclusion involves serious risks, and artistic creation adopts widely varying forms that occupy, quite legitimately, areas that while very different are nonetheless complementary. To travel in a single direction – except when driving down a one-way street – is in my view a great mistake. Diversity enriches by its own nature, and, this being so, art embraces an infinite variety of objects and effects for its own benefit. Orthodoxy, if we will, resides in the ideas and the method. Painting, as a medium, is the result of a mixture of diverse materials that provide, in their most basic application, texture and colour. In my opinion, systematic exclusion is a bad practice. Positive values are positive in themselves and not by the elimination of what we think unsuitable. The practice of exclusion, I think, can lead us to a sort of undesirable limitation. The grotesque is an art with its own personality, its own resources, and its wide-ranging registers. It could be argued that the grotesque represents, let us say, the chronicle of the unofficial version of the conventions that control our lives beyond even art itself. Or perhaps it is the hidden face that represents transgression. This, according to my way of seeing things, is equivalent to an appreciable and salutary exercise in freedom and imagination.

To see oneself reflected in a mirror, for example, is not sufficient since we know beforehand whom or what we are going to find there, and if it is not what we wanted to see we can have remedial recourse to cosmetics in order to become what at the moment we are not. This is similar to the function of the mask or disguise in carnival or theatrical iconography, and by extension in painting, which in itself is a reflection of these and other hidden phenomena. It may be debatable, but in an imagined world it is natural that only the imagination is really real. This apparent incongruity reminds us that, in these questions, one must tread warily because the nuances acquire an enormous importance. The grotesque, for example, is not, as is sometimes maintained, equivalent to the pathetic. The grotesque has been considered a classical and concrete allegorical style, and this means that the synonyms that have habitually been attributed to it are inadequate.

As I said at the beginning, my first attempts in painting were those natural and inevitable in the case of a youth absolutely ignorant of the medium and whose only desire was to somehow represent those elements he found within himself, alien to the external world. Given my introverted personality, painting provided me with the life-enhancing sensation that at last I was communicating with something, with somebody. This enthralled me to such an extent that I thought about it constantly. Books, as I also mentioned earlier, unlocked the doors of my imagination and, always attracted by mystery, I read particularly the fantastic tales generated by the Post-Romantics. This fascination for the unknown developed at the same time that I was discovering, as well as the classics, the painting of the Pre-Raphaelites, the Symbolists and, finally, that of the Surrealists, as well as their literature. All of this had a huge influence on my first period until I began to achieve a more personal work.

I suspect that from now on I will be engaged in a process of synthesis. What the future has in store for me I do not know, but what is certain is that I will keep painting in the same way as I started: this must be my destiny. And I still aspire to paint, one day, my best picture. What I have written here is what I habitually ponder in the solitude of my studio.

FIGURE 2.7. This photograph is still the same corner of my studio, where I live, where I receive my spiritual nutrition, where I still let myself be surprised every day, the studio which I have no plans to leave. Image appears by courtesy of the artist.

If I have managed, on this occasion, by means of words, to transmit my sentiments to you, believe me, this will indeed give me great pleasure. If, by chance, I have not, I must ask for your forgiveness.

3 Quantum beauty: real *and* ideal

FRANK WILCZEK

When I was asked to talk about quantum beauty I was a little startled, because the beauty of quantum theory is something that practising physicists, in the course of their work, rarely think about or mention. But when I gave the idea a chance, it really caught my imagination. And that's why I'm here. Quantum beauty really is a wonderful, true thing to talk about.

I'm going to sneak up on quantum beauty by putting it in historical context. The right context, I think, is a broader question:

Does the world embody beautiful ideas?

That is a question that people have thought about for a long time. Its intellectual history deserves volumes and syllabi. Here, though, I want to keep things brief and entertaining, so I shall spin a simple tale of heroes.

Pythagoras and Plato intuited that the world *should* embody beautiful ideas; Newton and Maxwell demonstrated how the world *could* embody beautiful ideas, in specific impressive cases. Finally, in the twentieth century in modern physics, and especially in quantum physics, we find a definitive answer: Yes! – the world *does* embody beautiful ideas.

Pythagorean beauty

According to Raphael, in his *School of Athens*, this is what Pythagoras looked like (Figure 3.1). You see he is writing something there. You have to squint to see exactly what, and when you do basically it's gibberish, but I like to pretend that he's documenting his famous credo 'All Things are Number'.

FIGURE 3.1. Pythagoras, as imagined by Raphael in his *School of Athens.*
Detail from Raphael (1483–1520): School of Athens: left-hand part (Empedocles,
Pythagoras, Francesco Maria della Rovere, Anaxagoras and Heraclitus under the semblance
of Michaelangelo). Vatican, Stanza della Segnatura. © 2013. Photo Scala, Florence.

It's hard to know at this distance in time exactly what Pythagoras had in
mind with that credo, but we can make a pretty good guess at its spirit.

Pythagoras, obviously, was very impressed by Pythagoras' theorem.
Pythagoras' theorem is a statement about right triangles. It tells you that
if you erect squares on the different sides, then the sum of the areas of the

FIGURE 3.2. Pythagoras (c. 580–500 BC) discovering the consonances of the octave from 'Theorica Musicae' by Franchino Gaffurio, first published in 1480, from 'Revue de l'Histoire du théâtre', 1959 (engraving) (b/w photo. French school, (20th century) / Bibliothèque des Arts Décoratifs, Paris, France / Archives Charmet / The Bridgeman Art Library.

two smaller squares adds up to the area of the largest square. Pythagoras' theorem is very familiar by now to most educated people, but when you really listen to its message afresh, with Pythagoras' ears so to speak, you realize that it is saying something quite startling. It is telling you that the *geometry* of objects embodies hidden *numerical* relationships. It says, in other words, that Number describes, if not yet everything, at least something very important about physical reality, namely the sizes and shapes of the objects that inhabit it.

Pythagoras is also responsible for another startling, impressive realization of the idea that 'All Things are Number'. In this much cruder representation (Figure 3.2), Pythagoras is exposing another of his great discoveries: if you pluck strings which are under tension by weights that are in simple numerical proportions (ratios of small whole numbers) and/ or strings stopped so that their lengths are in simple numerical proportions, then you get tones that sound pleasant together. We say they are in harmony. This is another startling relationship bridging Things – here the world of perception, of sound – and Number.

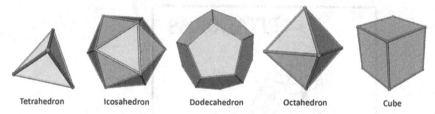

Tetrahedron   Icosahedron   Dodecahedron   Octahedron   Cube

FIGURE 3.3. The five Platonic solids. Image courtesy of Salvatore Torquato, Princeton University.

Platonic beauty

All this made a tremendous impression on Plato, and through Plato it was transmitted down the centuries. Plato, among many other things, is famous for the Platonic solids (Figure 3.3). These are solids whose faces are all identical regular polygons – in fact, equilateral triangles, squares, or regular pentagons. For later use, and also just because it is interesting, I'd like to say something about these remarkable objects. There are exactly five Platonic solids. There's the tetrahedron, which has four sides, each of which is an equilateral triangle. There's a wonderful shape, the icosahedron, built from twenty equilateral triangles coming together in groups of five. The dodecahedron, which will become our friend later in this chapter, has twelve sides, all pentagonal. There's the familiar cube, and the octahedron, and that's it – just these five shapes, no more and no less. Euclid's *Elements* ends with the construction of these Platonic solids, and many people conjecture that Euclid intended that to be an appropriate climax to his work.

That requiring symmetry can pin down a few specific, discrete possibilities for structure was a striking discovery. It inspired Plato to propose a Theory of Everything that, while primitive, is very much in the spirit of modern ideas, as we will see. Plato proposed that the different building-blocks of nature, the elements, of which at that time there were thought to be four (earth, air, fire, water), are made out of atoms, each having the shape of one of the Platonic solids. The icosahedron is left over, and Plato proposed that it is the shape of the universe as a whole. I can't accept Plato's theory in detail, but the idea that there are exactly five things that you can use to construct the world, and that these things embody mathematical principles, is a remarkable kind of intuition.

FIGURE 3.4. Plato's metaphor of the cave. Those who rely exclusively on their senses are like spectators of a shadow puppet show; they see only the projection of a richer reality. Image courtesy of Scott Mayhew.

Plato also described a more philosophical concept that is central to our question. This is his metaphor of the cave (Figure 3.4). According to this metaphor, as human beings we perceive not ultimate reality, but only a sort of projection: mere shadows on the wall of a cave. Plato's message here was that the world at its most fundamental level could embody beauty, despite paltry (or messy) appearances. One of our goals as thinkers, philosophers, or just appreciators of the world should be to imagine, from the projections we perceive, what the real thing is. Plato believed that the real thing would be more perfect, and more beautiful, and more spacious than the projection. Yet there must be a precise mapping from the underlying reality to the projection, and that is how you can test and refine your ideas about what the underlying reality is.

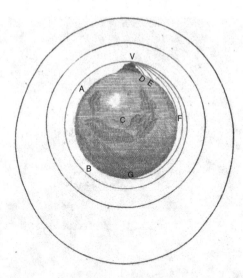

FIGURE 3.5. Newton's thought-experiment relating the motion of projectiles to the orbits of astronomical bodies. From Isaac Newton, *A Treatise of the System of the World* (London, 1728).

Newtonian beauty

The ancients gave us hopes and philosophical ideas for how beauty might be embodied in the physical world, and a few splendid examples. Those hopes and very partial insights became much more impressive when Cambridge started to get into the act. Here, from Newton's *Principia*, is my favourite diagram in the whole literature of science (Figure 3.5). You have to imagine someone on top of a mountain throwing a stone horizontally, harder and harder. And it is clear, intuitively, what should happen. The stone will go further and further. And eventually, if you throw it hard enough, it comes all the way back! Then you can imagine a higher mountain. There would also be closed orbits – possible motions of the thrown object – starting from those higher peaks. And you begin to see from this thought-experiment, without any equation or elaborate mathematics, the emergent idea that gravity could be a universal force. The same force can be responsible for how projectiles move close to the surface of the Earth, and how the Moon orbits the Earth – or, by extension, how Galileo's moons of Jupiter orbit Jupiter, or both planets

FIGURE 3.6. Breaking white light into its component parts, and reconstructing it. Image courtesy of Michael W. Davidson and Kirill I. Tchourioukanov.

orbit the Sun. Another aspect of Newton's theory of motion, which leaps out of this diagram, is that orbiting is no different from falling. The stone, even when it is orbiting, is still falling. But because it is falling towards a moving target, so to speak, it never hits the surface. It just keeps falling without ever getting closer to the ground.

Newton also famously introduced the idea he called 'analysis and synthesis', basically what we now call 'reductionism'. More accurately I should not say that Newton introduced reductionism, but rather that Newton provided such impressive examples that analysis and synthesis, as a method, became the default strategy of fundamental science. The way to understand light in particular, but by an analogy potentially everything in the physical world, according to Newton, is to break it down into its most minute components (Figure 3.6). A prism breaks any kind of light, for example sunlight, into its component pure colours. But then to show that these beams are the fundamental components of light, you have to show that they cannot be broken down further, which Newton checked in other beautiful experiments. And that you can use them to build back up the white light, which he also did.

This is what Newton looked like when he was making these discoveries as a young man, according to William Blake (Figure 3.7). You see he was very fit, and most comfortable in the buff. But the most important message of this image, the message that Blake took from Newton and meant to convey, is the idea that the world is constructed according to precise constructions of a mathematical nature, and that we should be ambitious in trying to find precisely what they are. It is the message of Plato's cave, but the metaphor has been fleshed out, and there's a new confidence: we *can* get from shadows to substance, and the 'substance' we discover is mathematical law, or in other words ideal concepts.

FIGURE 3.7. Newton constructing a mathematical world, as imagined by William Blake. William Blake, Newton, 1795/c.1805, by Tate / Digital Image © Tate, London 2011.

Maxwellian beauty

These are Maxwell's equations (Figure 3.8). First written in the 1860s, they summarized everything that was known about electricity and magnetism at that time plus one more effect, the entry in the box, which was Maxwell's original contribution. Maxwell introduced this term, which says that changing electric fields produce magnetic fields, because when he put together all the other equations describing the phenomena that were known at the time, he discovered an inconsistency. So something had to change. Now the way Maxwell came to his term was by constructing an elaborate mechanical model ('constructed', of course, in his mind!) that supported the same forces and flows of energy as the electric and magnetic fields. His model, because it was constructed according to sound Newtonian mechanics, could not be

Maxwell's Equations

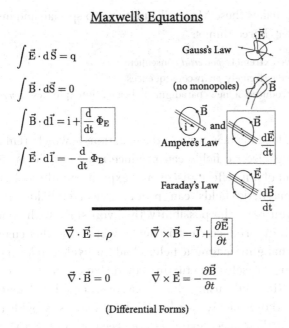

$$\int \vec{E} \cdot d\vec{S} = q \qquad \text{Gauss's Law}$$

$$\int \vec{B} \cdot d\vec{S} = 0 \qquad \text{(no monopoles)}$$

$$\int \vec{B} \cdot d\vec{l} = i + \frac{d}{dt}\Phi_E$$

$$\int \vec{E} \cdot d\vec{l} = -\frac{d}{dt}\Phi_B$$

Ampère's Law

Faraday's Law

$$\vec{\nabla} \cdot \vec{E} = \rho \qquad \vec{\nabla} \times \vec{B} = \vec{J} + \frac{\partial \vec{E}}{\partial t}$$

$$\vec{\nabla} \cdot \vec{B} = 0 \qquad \vec{\nabla} \times \vec{E} = -\frac{\partial \vec{B}}{\partial t}$$

(Differential Forms)

FIGURE 3.8. The Maxwell equations in integral, differential and pictorial forms.

inconsistent. But when he analysed it carefully, Maxwell saw that his imaginative mechanical model of electric and magnetic fields contained the new effect, and so working backwards he proposed that real, physical electric and magnetic fields must have it as well. Very Platonic! And to this day, the equations Maxwell wrote down in 1864 are the foundation of our understanding of the phenomena of electricity and magnetism and much else.

Heinrich Hertz, the experimentalist who verified some of the surprising predictions of Maxwell's equations twenty-five years later, and in so doing invented radio, said something about the Maxwell equations that I find beautiful and poetic, and also true and very relevant:

> One cannot escape the feeling that these mathematical formulae have an independent existence and an intelligence of their own, that they are wiser than we are, wiser even than their discoverers, that we get more out of them than was originally put into them.

What is it that makes these Maxwell equations so special, and inspired Hertz's rhapsody[1]? Three things:

- They have extremely *powerful* consequences
- They have extremely *pretty* consequences
- They introduced a new paradigm of beauty into physics: *symmetry of equations*

Before Maxwell added his new term to the equations – which, remember, said that changing electric fields can produce magnetic fields – there was already a kind of dual effect, discovered experimentally by Faraday, that changing magnetic fields can produce electric fields. Putting them together, you have the possibility that you start with changing magnetic fields, they produce electric fields, which are also changing, so they produce changing magnetic fields. And the cycle can keep going, thereby producing a self-perpetuating disturbance that can move through space. Maxwell, using his equations, could calculate the speed at which those newly predicted disturbances would travel. He discovered that their speed matched the speed of light. So Maxwell, being a very clever fellow, made the leap that 'we can scarcely avoid the inference that light consists in the transverse undulations of the same medium which is the cause of electric and magnetic phenomena'. And to this day, that is our theory of what light is, at the deepest level. It is those disturbances in electric and magnetic fields, which spin out of Maxwell's equations.

Powerful indeed! But there's much more – even much more than bringing light within the purview of electricity and magnetism. For there are possibilities for disturbances of different wavelengths – in Maxwell's theory, different rates of changing electric into magnetic fields. Visible light corresponds to only a limited range of wavelengths, with Newton's beams of pure colours each representing some specific wavelength. That is basically what was known at the time of Maxwell. But the equations have more solutions. Hertz eventually produced waves of much longer wavelength, which have become famous as radio. Infrared and ultraviolet

---

[1] If you look in the other writings of Hertz, you find that normally he's quite restrained and professorial.

FIGURE 3.9. The shadow of a razor's edge, cast in monochromatic light, viewed at high resolution.

radiation, microwaves, X-rays, gamma rays – all those mainstays of modern technology and astronomy – they are all contained in Maxwell's equations.

When you solve them, you find that Maxwell's equations give you beautiful structures. I will not be able to do justice here to the beauty of essentially mathematical phenomena. But since the solutions describe tangible realities, I can show you the beautiful tangible reality instead! Here is the shadow projected by a razor blade, or anything with a sharp straight edge, when illuminated by pure light (Figure 3.9). And you see that the shadow is not merely the absence of light. Formal geometric reasoning, based on the crude idea that light strictly travels in straight lines, would have told you the shadow is a sharp division between darkness and light. But when we calculate the disturbances in electric and magnetic fields that Maxwell taught us light really is, we find there is a lot more structure. It is a beautiful, very precisely calculable structure that you can get from the Maxwell equations, and nowadays with bright monochromatic lasers available you can compare the prediction directly with reality. Looking at this thing you just have to say: Isn't that pretty?

Most profoundly for the future of physics, Maxwell's equations introduced an essentially new idea, which had not really played a big role in science before, and which has become more and more dominant in our attempts to guess new laws of nature: the idea that *equations* can have symmetry. And, moreover, that the equations nature likes have lots of symmetry.

What does it mean, to say that equations have symmetry? While the word has various, often vague, meanings in everyday life, in mathematics *symmetry* means something quite precise. It means change without change. Spelling out that Delphic formulation: we say an object is symmetric if we can make transformations on it that might have changed it but in fact do not. So for instance a circle is very symmetric because you can rotate a circle around its centre, and though every point on it moves, overall it remains the same circle; whereas if you took some more lopsided shape and rotated it, you would always get something different.

The same idea can be applied to equations. Here's a simple equation

$$x = y$$

which you can see is neatly balanced between x and y. You would be tempted to say that it is symmetric. And indeed it is, according to the mathematical definition. For if you change x into y and y into x, you get a different equation, namely

$$y = x$$

But the new equation has exactly the same content as the old one, so we have change without change: symmetry. Whereas, say, $x = y + 2$ changes into $y = x + 2$, which is not the same thing at all, so that equation is not symmetric. Symmetry is a property that certain equations, or by extension systems of equations, have while others do not.

Maxwell's equations, it turns out, have an enormous amount of symmetry. There are several families of transformations you can make on Maxwell's equations, that change their form but not their overall content. You can change space into time, if you do it in the right way. That possibility is the essence of the theory of special relativity – which, historically, arose from thinking about Maxwell's equations. You can also change electric fields into magnetic fields, if you do it in the right way.

In modern physics we have learned to work towards truth in the opposite direction, reversing Maxwell's path. Instead of using experiments to infer equations, and then finding to our delight and astonishment that the equations have a lot of symmetry, we propose equations with enormous symmetry and then check to see whether nature uses them. It has been an amazingly successful strategy.

The quantum beauty of matter

With that background, we are well prepared to appreciate the beauty of the quantum world.

The quantum description of atoms realizes Pythagoras' vision uncannily. The mathematics of electrons in atoms is exactly the same mathematics that people developed to describe musical instruments. The equations for vibrations of the air within a woodwind instrument, specifically, bear a strong family resemblance to the equations we use to describe the motion of electrons in atoms. When the woodwind is sounding a pure tone, inside it there is a space-dependent pattern of density and pressure that oscillates in time. We call it a standing wave. In the quantum atom, the nature of the waves that vibrate is a little (actually, a lot) more abstract. They are waves of probability amplitude, and the things that oscillate one into the other are the real and imaginary parts of the wave functions. It would require a long digression to spell all that out from scratch, so suffice it to say that the equations are basically the same. In the early days of quantum mechanics, when physicists were developing these equations and learning how to solve them, one of the main textbooks on the mathematics of quantum theory was actually Lord Rayleigh's classic textbook *The Theory of Sound*.

Let us consider for example the simplest atom – the hydrogen atom – and ask what the electron wave patterns look like when the electron is in one of its stable states (Figure 3.10).

These so-called stationary states are the analogue of pure tones for the musical instrument. This picture shows two-dimensional sections of what the stationary states look like. I think you will agree they are aesthetic-ally attractive. And the more you know, the more profoundly attractive they become, as you understand that they are the solution of precise mathematical equations, whose consequences have been checked down to the ninth decimal place. Nor do the two-dimensional projections do them justice; they have a lot of internal spatial structure. Here's a cut-away

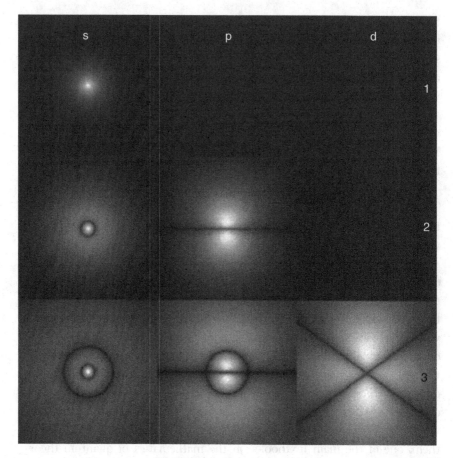

FIGURE 3.10. Two-dimensional projections of the wave functions for stationary states of electrons in hydrogen.

view of one particular orbital (Figure 3.11). It's wonderful to think that inside us, as our substance, we find structure that is fabulously intricate and pretty to visualize, that embodies precise equations whose consequences we can check in fantastic detail.

In the limited space available I will not be able to do anything remotely approaching full justice to the beauty of quantum mechanics revealed in the description of matter and the many phenomena of chemistry. I will just give you a taste by way of a sampler from one particularly relatively simple, yet dramatic, corner of the subject, namely the chemistry of pure carbon.

FIGURE 3.11. Cross-section showing the internal structure of one particular stationary state. (For experts: (421).) © Bernd Thaller, 2004.

In a hydrogen atom there is one proton and one electron. That electron is bound to the proton and forms patterns that are centred on that proton. If you have a situation with many nuclei – many concentrations of positive charges that are attractive to electrons – the electrons find efficient ways to play the field. Since all the electrons are the same, and (since we are dealing with pure carbon) all the nuclei are the same, and arranged in a regular crystal-like (i.e. symmetric) pattern, we will find the same tricks used over and over again.

The electrons arrange their wave functions according to simple principles that follow directly from the equations of quantum theory. Each carbon atom has four electrons to dispose of. There are two especially symmetric ways for these four electrons to arrange themselves, and these, as you might have guessed, turn out to be the most efficient arrangements. One way is for three of them to point symmetrically to the vertices of an equilateral triangle. To be more precise, the wave functions are partly concentrated on a central carbon atom, but the region of high density is shaped like a little cigar, and the cigars point out in different directions, towards the vertices of an equilateral triangle. The payoff is that there can be another carbon nucleus at the other end of the cigar, and then the electron gets to flirt both with its original mate and with that other one. Three electrons from each carbon atom reach out that way, towards the corners of an equilateral triangle, and the fourth wanders off into the transverse direction. That is one efficient arrangement. The other is to have the four electrons in orbits that point towards the vertices of a regular tetrahedron – one of Plato's ideally symmetric arrangements, the Platonic solid with four vertices, you might recall.

Nature exploits these efficient arrangements with exuberant flair and, I'd say, a certain jovial humour. I shall show you some pictures that demonstrate those points quite convincingly. But first I want to emphasize that there are equations and experiments that go with the pretty pictures. One of the nice things about quantum beauty is the better you understand it, the more beautiful it seems. (With other kinds of beauty, like the beauty of magic and ceremony, that is not always the case, unfortunately.)

Here is an arrangement in which you have the cigar-orbitals making the equilateral triangle kind of connections everywhere, over and over again (Figure 3.12). This the so-called buckyball, or buckminsterfullerene molecule, which is a dodecahedron-like object. A literal dodecahedron isn't quite flat enough; the four neighbouring carbon atoms do not lie in a plane, and the favourable orbital arrangement is too compromised to be stable. But you can flesh out a dodecahedron with as many hexagons as you like, it turns out, consistent with the rule that each carbon atom reaches out to three near neighbours. The buckyball is a particularly stable form that contains 60 carbon atoms, forming exactly 12 pentagons

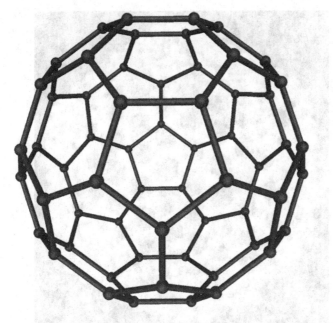

FIGURE 3.12. The C-60 molecule, also known as the 'buckyball'. Created by Michael Stock.

(as in the parent dodecahedron) and the rest hexagons. Its existence was a great discovery that won the Nobel Prize in chemistry for the discoverers.

I should mention that these buckyballs, and their relatives, are components of soot – the black rubbish that is left over when you burn carbon inefficiently. You see there is great beauty hidden in soot, when you view it with the mind's eye. We must imagine Plato smiling.

You can keep going with these ideas. Here is a molecule constructed that has been made with 540 carbon atoms, obeying the same basic principles, and making a very impressive, large sphere (Figure 3.13). You can try to put things inside the sphere, and transport them around in that nice organic cage. This could have practical applications, for instance in drug delivery, as you can keep an active molecule sequestered until it arrives where it is wanted.

The ultimate in this kind of planar symmetry is a true two-dimensional flat plane, extending those equilateral triangle arrangements indefinitely (Figure 3.14). This describes the substance called graphene. Graphene

FIGURE 3.13. A giant molecule of pure carbon, with near-planar bonding.

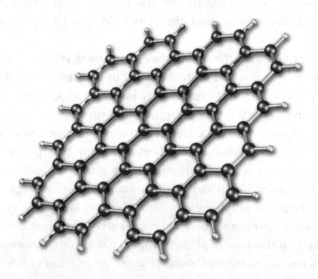

FIGURE 3.14. The ultimate in planar carbon: graphene. Image courtesy of Lawrence Berkeley Laboratory.

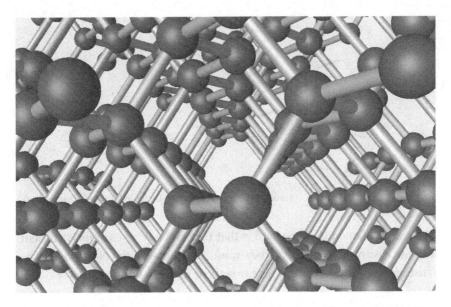

FIGURE 3.15. Diamond: a crystal of pure carbon with tetrahedral bonding. http://www.crystmol.com/crystalstructures.html. The figure produced using CrystMol.

was first isolated in the pure form in 2004. That achievement was recognized with the 2010 Nobel Prize in physics, awarded to Andre Geim and Konstantin Novoselov. Remarkably, the properties of this material had been worked out in great detail long before, in the late 1940s. The definiteness of the equations of quantum theory, and the simple symmetry of the solutions relevant to graphene, allowed physicists to predict the properties of graphene in advance, and to make rapid progress towards exploiting it once it was isolated.

You can also fold up ribbons of graphene, to make tubes. These are called nanotubes. Because you can start with ribbons of different width, and also introduce twists before reconnecting, nanotubes come in many varieties. Nanotubes that are only slightly different geometrically turn out to have extremely different properties – some conduct electricity beautifully while others are insulators, for example. The world of nanotubes is a wonderful playground both for mathematics and for technology.

The three-dimensional symmetric arrangement – where the electrons reach out to the different vertices of a tetrahedron – makes diamond (Figure 3.15).

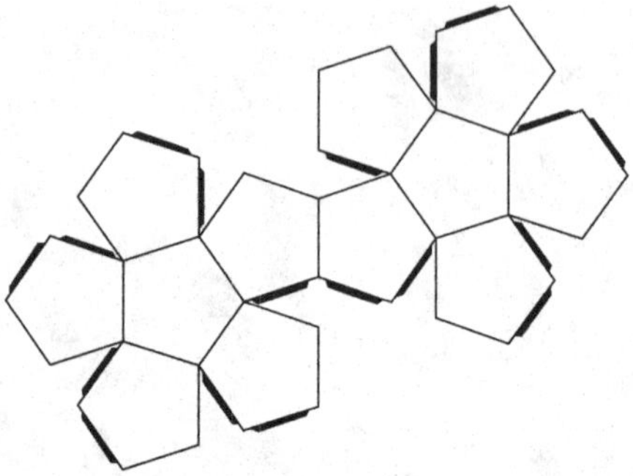

FIGURE 3.16. An object that is begging to be folded into a dodecahedron.

The reason diamonds are so hard is that they embody an extremely efficient way for electrons to do what they want. And because the electrons are so satisfied, it is very difficult to persuade them to break up their network.

The quantum beauty of unification

I could go on with many, many other beautiful examples from chemistry, but I want to conclude by describing a current frontier of understanding – or maybe misunderstanding – in our exploration of quantum beauty. As I hinted briefly before, the big idea is that in theoretical physics we have gone from *observing* symmetry in equations that experiments lead us to, to *proposing* equations with enormous symmetry, and asking nature's verdict on them. In other words we are trying to use beauty actively, as our guiding principle, rather than as something we observe passively. We have become artists, but artists with a difference: we voluntarily submit our work to a hopefully loving but in any case unimpeachable critic, Mother Nature.

Consider again the dodecahedron. It is perhaps most familiar as a calendar. It is very convenient for that use, having twelve sides that are nice and equal, so you can fit a month on each one. A dodecahedron is interesting to look at, and by now it is becoming our friend. And so if we stumbled on this unlabelled object (Figure 3.16) on the internet, we would recognize what it is, or rather what it is meant to be. Look, it has twelve pentagons – twelve regular pentagons, partially connected. Obviously, this is an object that is meant to be folded up into a dodecahedron.

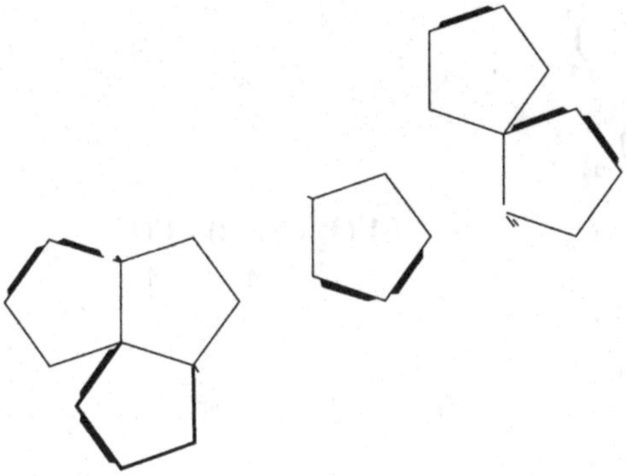

FIGURE 3.17. When the object is partially obscured, its meaning is less obvious.

But suppose some evil spirit erased part of an unfolded dodecahedron, to make this mystery object. (Figure 3.17). Now it gets harder to recognize what it should be. Most people, perhaps not having thought about dodecahedra recently, wouldn't know what to make of that peculiar thing. But if you remembered about regular solids and dodecahedra you might say well, it is very special that we have pentagons, and that they are connected in this particular way, so I guess what this is meant to be is a dodecahedron, but somebody has erased part of it. Brilliant deduction! Keep that in mind.

And now we turn to the Standard Model of particle physics. It describes an enormous wealth of facts – hard, quantitative realities about the physical world – in a very compact set of equations. I will not remotely be able to do justice to what these equations are, nor their details. But I hope you will trust me that almost everything we know about physics is encoded honestly in Figure 3.18, if you know how to decode it. And the decoding does not require putting in extra information or fudge factors or anything of that sort, but just spelling out the logic of the symbols.

A central pillar of the Standard Model is the idea of gauge symmetry. Gauge symmetry is a principle that was discovered in connection with the Maxwell equations, and has been vastly generalized since then. For present purposes, the important point is that equations of the Standard Model have symmetries that can change many of its particles one into another. In our diagram, all the particles within each bracket are related by symmetries of the equations.

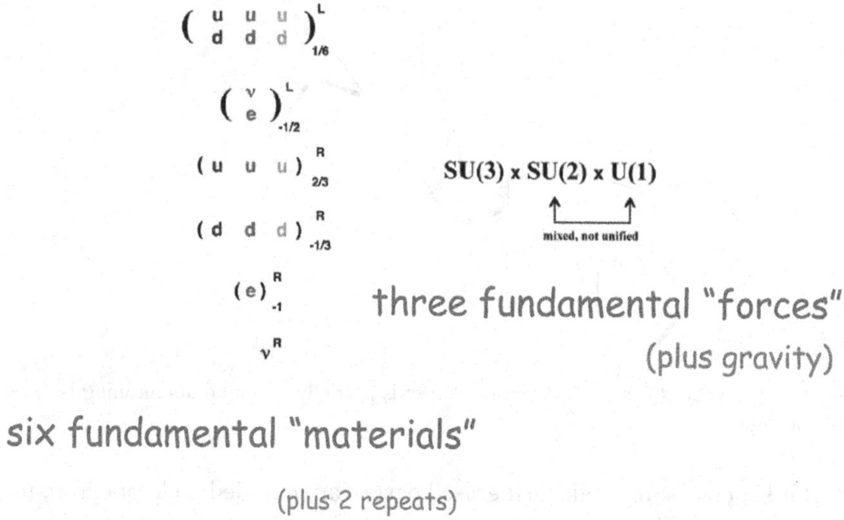

Frank Wilczek

$$\left(\begin{smallmatrix} u & u & u \\ d & d & d \end{smallmatrix} \right)^{L}_{1/6}$$

$$\left(\begin{smallmatrix} \nu \\ e \end{smallmatrix} \right)^{L}_{-1/2}$$

$$(u \quad u \quad u)^{R}_{2/3}$$

$$(d \quad d \quad d)^{R}_{-1/3}$$

$$(e)^{R}_{-1}$$

$$\nu^{R}$$

SU(3) x SU(2) x U(1)

↑   ↑

mixed, not unified

three fundamental "forces"

(plus gravity)

six fundamental "materials"

(plus 2 repeats)

FIGURE 3.18. Structure of the Standard Model of fundamental physics.

Thus, although there are a lot of particles that go into this description of physics, in a strong sense many of them are just different aspects of the same particle. If two particles are related by symmetry – if one is transformed into the other – they really should not be thought of as separate, independent elements of reality. Symmetry tells you that as those particles transform one into the other, the content of the equations has to stay the same. If the transformed equations are going to have the same content, the particle that an existing particle transforms into had better also exist, and have equivalent properties. If you have one, and symmetry, you have the other.

The Standard Model is a very powerful, very compact framework. It would be difficult, as I said, to exaggerate its precision, its power and – when you spell it out properly – its beauty. But physicists are not satisfied. Just because the Standard Model is so close to nature's last word, we should judge it by high standards, and try to reconstruct its hidden beauties (remembering the lesson of Plato's cave).

Scrutinized in that spirit, the Standard Model challenges us to do better. It contains three mathematically similar but independent forces: the strong, weak, and electromagnetic interactions. (Gravity is a fourth force, superficially of a very different character from the others; we will come back to it shortly.) We would like to have one unifying force that really underlies everything in a coherent description of nature. Three (or four) is more than one, so we are not there yet. Even worse, even after declaring different particles related by symmetry to be a single entity, we are left with six unrelated 'fundamental' entities, and six is also definitely more than one.

So we would like to do better. It is as if we have been presented with that partial realization of a dodecahedron, with something erased. The mathematics of the possible symmetries of objects in space led us to a few Platonic solids, and let us infer an underlying dodecahedron from partial, distorted evidence. Can we do something similar with the gauge symmetry we find in the equations of fundamental physics?

Needless to say, I would not be leading you down this path unless we could. There are only a few possibilities for symmetries that perfect the gauge symmetry of the Standard Model, just as there are only a few Platonic solids. We can try them out, and see whether any of them fit the bill. And one of the possible symmetries seems to fit the known particles and extend the structure of the Standard Model most beautifully (Figure 3.19). (For experts: it is based on the group SO(10) and its spinor representation.) If you expand the equations this way, then all the forces can be transformed one into the other, as can all the particles. So, as I just argued, we really have just one force and one particle. Awesome!

But when you examine this idea a little more closely, it seems to have a fatal flaw. If we are going to have symmetry among the different forces, then those forces have to have the same strength. As we observe them, however, they do not. The strong interaction really is stronger than the other interactions. The three interactions are definitely *not* equal in strength.

Having come this far, however, we should not give up too easily. Maybe here too we need to heed the lesson of Plato's cave, and think beyond the superficial appearance of things.

A great insight of the last part of the twentieth century is that what we ordinarily perceive as empty space appears, in our fundamental description of nature, to be far from empty. It is as if we are fish who have finally realized that they are immersed in a medium – water, of

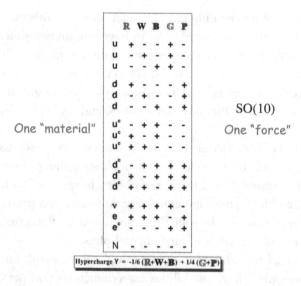

	R	W	B	G	P
u	+	-	-	+	-
u	-	+	-	+	-
u	-	-	+	+	-
d	+	-	-	-	+
d	-	+	-	-	+
d	-	-	+	-	+
u^c	-	+	+	-	-
u^c	+	-	+	-	-
u^c	+	+	-	-	-
d^c	-	+	+	+	+
d^c	+	-	+	+	+
d^c	+	+	-	+	+
v	+	+	+	+	-
e	+	+	+	-	+
e^c	-	-	-	+	+
N	-	-	-	-	-

One "material"

SO(10)

One "force"

Hypercharge Y = -1/6 (R+W+B) + 1/4 (G+P)

FIGURE 3.19. A unified theory of the building-blocks of matter and of the standard model forces.

course – that they have taken for granted until now. We have learned that you can get a better description of nature by recognizing that you are in a medium that has its own properties.

This is what your eyes would see if they could have resolution in time of 10^{-24} seconds and resolution in space of 10^{-14} centimetres – really, really small and really, really fast (Figure 3.20). But for your convenience in viewing, I have blown it up and taken a snapshot. This picture, based on hard calculation, shows fluctuations in the energy and gluon fields in quantum chromodynamics (QCD), our theory of quarks and gluons. Since QCD has been tested quantitatively with almost incredible rigour, it is as certain as anything can be in science that this picture accurately depicts what is happening in the microworld.

Just as water distorts the perception of fish, the medium of space distorts our vision of fundamental processes. Now we realize that correcting for that distortion might be a very good thing to do. The forces as we observe them do not appear amenable to unification; but to see things as they really are, more basically, we need to strip away the distorting effects of the medium.

FIGURE 3.20. The fluctuating distribution of gluon field energy in space, viewed at high spatial and time resolution. The brightest colours are regions of highest energy density. Regions of very low energy density have been made completely devoid of colour, allowing access to view through 'empty' regions of space. For the colour image, see www.darwin.cam.ac.uk/lectures/beauty. Image courtesy of Derek Leinweber, CSSM, University of Adelaide.

We can do that with the stroke of a pen. There is no problem to calculate the requisite corrections, and thereby to get a cleared-up view of what is happening at much shorter distances (Figure 3.21). As you can see, this strategy almost works – the three lines representing the strengths of the different forces almost meet in a point – but not quite. (The width of the lines indicates the experimental and theoretical uncertainties.)

Now if we followed the famous philosopher Karl Popper we could be happy at this point. Karl Popper taught that the goal of science was to produce falsifiable theories, and now we have produced a theory that is not merely falsifiable, but outright false. What could be better than that?

But of course that is not the way we think about it. We had a beautiful idea that seemed promising, and almost worked. Such ideas are precious,

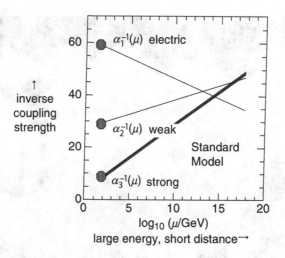

FIGURE 3.21. Near-miss for unification, after making corrections to account for fluctuating fields in space.

so we should not give up too easily. In the spirit of youth and audacity, let me suggest[2] that perhaps we have not been quite bold enough.

In our hypothetical unification we have united the description of the basic ingredients of matter, including electrons and quarks. They have very different properties, but in the unified theory they are different aspects of a single entity, viewed from different but equivalent perspectives. Similarly the forces, or if you like the force-transmitting particles such as photons and gluons, were unified. We got down to one kind of force-transmitting entity and one kind of matter-making entity. But that is still two things, and two is more than one. So the obvious audacious question is: Can we connect those two remaining kinds of things – particles and forces – by some sort of symmetry?

Well, for a long time that was thought to be difficult or impossible, and then just impossible. But in the 1970s several physicists, led by Julius Wess and Bruno Zumino, developed another powerful unifying idea: supersymmetry (SUSY). The central idea of supersymmetry is that there are new quantum dimensions, beyond the familiar dimensions of

[2] As I first did in 1981, when 'youth' was a better fit.

space–time. A quantum dimension is radically different from a conventional dimension. (For experts: while the coordinates of ordinary space are ordinary real numbers, the coordinates of quantum dimensions are Grassman numbers, which satisfy $xy = -yx$.) If a particle moves off into a quantum dimension it does not change its position, in the usual sense; instead it changes into a different kind of particle! Matter-making kinds of particles turn into force-transmitting particles, and vice versa. More technically, we say that fermions transform into bosons, and vice versa, when they step into superspace. So if supersymmetry is right, then parallel to the ordinary plane of existence we have the super world, where electrons turn into selectrons, a spin zero version of electrons; gluons turn into gluinos, a sort of matter version of gluons; and so forth. And now by flipping those two planes, if the equations of the world are supersymmetric, we will get different equations where the partner particles have changed one into the other. But if those equations have symmetry – in other words, if supersymmetry is a true feature of the physical world – the new equations will have the same content as the old ones.

That next level of unification doesn't come for free. We have had to postulate the existence of a new world: the world where we arrive when we step into superspace. We have to make bigger equations that make use of that new world and make it symmetric with the part of space we already know. We need those new selectrons, and gluinos, and so forth.

Those new particles also exist in fluctuating form, as virtual particles, stirring up the structure of space, further distorting our vision. We have to re-calculate our corrections, to take account of these additional distortions. And here a wonderful surprise emerges (Figure 3.22). Once you put in those additional corrections, the different interactions really do come together and unify accurately.[3]

And as an unexpected bonus to this, gravity – which started out horrendously weaker than the other forces, so on my plot it would start way outside the known universe – comes roaring in at extremely high energies, and manages also to unify with the other interactions pretty nearly.

---

[3] If you complete the equations in a fully consistent manner, the interactions will not un-unify at still shorter distances. Once they come together, they stick together.

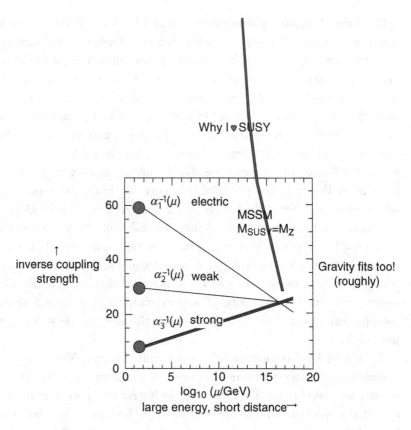

FIGURE 3.22. When we include the effect of the hypothetical particles required by supersymmetry, we find accurate unification.

So that, to my view, is how the frontier of our approach to understanding the deep structure of physical reality – realizing the dreams of Pythagoras and Plato, building on the insights of Newton and Maxwell – looks today. I think you will agree that the prospects are tantalizing.

But can we explore that frontier, not only with our minds, but physically? We can, and we will. If SUSY's new particles are going to support enough fluctuations to enable unification, they cannot be too heavy. If they exist, and are light enough to do the job, they will be produced and detected at the new Large Hadron Collider (LHC) – a fantastic undertaking at the CERN laboratory, near Geneva, just now coming into operation. There will be a trial by fire.

Will the particles SUSY requires reveal themselves?

If not, we will have the satisfaction of knowing we have done our job, according to Popper, by producing a falsifiable theory and showing that it is false.

But another possibility is that when we analyse the pictures of what has been produced at the LHC, we will discover that while most of it (by far) is stuff that has already incorporated in the Standard Model, once in a while, perhaps once in a billion or once in a trillion events, there will be something additional, that does not conform to the Standard Model – another kind of particle. You have to sift through a lot of hay to find the needle in the haystack, so you have to be very good at recognizing hay, and it's a tough business, but after a lot of analysis we might decode that through their properties the new particles are speaking to us, announcing 'I'm a selectron', 'I'm a gluino', and so forth. And then our visions of unification will have reached a new level of truth and vindication, and a new world will have been discovered. Soon we will know, one way or the other.

4 The sound of beauty

ELIZABETH EVA LEACH

The dangers associated with the sound of beauty are all too apparent in one of the earliest texts in the Western literary canon. On his way back from the Trojan war Odysseus is able to hear one of the most famous sounds of beauty in literature: the song of the sirens. Unlike the unfortunate sailors who had gone before him, however, cunning Odysseus is prepared. Earlier in the story, Circe had given him a detailed warning about the trials to come.

> First you will come to the Sirens, who beguile all mortals, any who comes their way. Whoso draws near in ignorance and hears the sound of the Sirens, him wife and innocent children shall not meet on his returning home, nor shall they have joy of him, but the Sirens beguile him with clear-voiced song, sitting in their meadow; but all about is a great heap of the bones of rotting men, and their hides waste away around them. But make speed past them, and knead honey-sweet wax and smear it over your comrades' ears, lest any of them should hear; but if you yourself wish to hear, let them bind you in the swift ship hand and foot, upright at the foot of the mast, and let cords be attached to you, so that you may hear the two Sirens' voice with pleasure. But if you beseech your comrades and bid them release you, let them bind you then with all the more bonds.
>
> (*Odyssey* book 12, lines 39–54)[1]

The wise Odysseus, famed for his cunning, obeys these instructions to the letter and gets to hear the song of the sirens in safety. Unlike every traveller who had gone before him, Odysseus experiences the sound of irresistibly enticing beauty and lives to tell the tale.

---

[1] Translation Leofranc Holford-Strevens, 'Sirens in Antiquity and the Middle Ages', in Linda P. Austern and Inna Naroditskaya (eds.), *Music of the Sirens* (Bloomington: Indiana University Press, 2006), 16–51, 16.

Deadly sonic beauty: the sound of the sirens

This tale makes explicit the link between the beauty of a song and its ability to overcome reason, to enchant, to beguile, its power to lead men astray and, ultimately, to their deaths. Sonic beauty's ability to kill the unwary – metaphorically or literally – serves as a powerful argument on one side of the coin of music's ethical value. This chapter explores both negative and positive understandings of the beauty of sound from Antiquity to the present, with a focus in particular on the later Middle Ages, which was the point when antique views of music were synthesized with Christian morality in a way that has arguably remained current ever since. What will emerge is a history of varied human judgements of music, arguments over the ethics of music's power, and arguments over music's place in defining what individual humanity is.

First, at our own peril, it is worth spending a little more time with the sirens. Reading book 12 of the *Odyssey* might well induce a curiosity as to what the sirens' song was actually like. What makes it so compellingly beautiful? But of course the power of this song lies partly in the fact that, except for Odysseus, no one – not even the narrator of the *Odyssey* – has heard it. If the narrator of the *Odyssey* (whom, for the sake of convenience, I shall call Homer) had heard it, he would not have been around to write the poem. And if it could be replicated directly, any audience of Homer's poem – itself a kind of song – would be running the same risk of death as the mariners. Effectively, the *Odyssey*'s second-hand reporting of the episode acts as the wax in its own audience's ears. The text simply calls the song 'clear', which might purely be a reflection of how comprehensible its words are, because this is not only beautiful music, but beautiful music with words – that is, song. Moreover, we are told what the words of the song are.

> Come hither, much-praised Odysseus, great glory of the Achaeans, draw up your ship, that you may hear the voice of us two. For no-one yet has passed this way in his black ship before hearing the honeyed voice from our mouths, but he goes home having rejoiced and knowing more. For we know all the things that in broad Troy the Argives and Trojans endured by the will of the gods.[2]

[2] Ibid., 17.

The sirens' song flatteringly tempts Odysseus with the retelling of the story of his own heroic role in the *Iliad*: classicists attest to how euphonious these lines are in the original Greek, and how close to the *Iliad* in diction.[3] If the hero is to leave Troy behind, however, he has to leave it behind in song as well as merely travelling away from it by boat; he has to reject the twin distractions of beauty and the warrior's glory carried together in the words and melody of the sirens' song if he is to return to the quotidian domesticity of Ithaca.

Beautiful sound causes the individual subject – Odysseus – to confront a conflict between desire and discipline. Only by being ready for the performance, by setting up a situation of self-control that is actually beyond his self-control, can Odysseus allow himself safely to experience what it feels like to lose control, to be free of oneself. Beautiful music defeats reason, removes self-control, and is therefore mortally dangerous. Only by binding oneself tightly to an upright mast and surrounding oneself by those deaf to music's pleasures can one survive the jeopardy that beautiful sound represents.

The argument that follows here explores some of the manifold ways in which music theory and musical practice have attempted – not always with great success – to provide the ropes that might allow the human subject to wallow in music's beauty while avoiding its dangers.

Transcendent sonic beauty

The dangerous sirens of the *Odyssey* were not the only ones in Antiquity: they can be contrasted with the sirens in the story of Er. At the end of Plato's *Republic* Socrates says that he will tell a story and notes that this story is specifically not one of the tales that Odysseus tells Alcinous (the tales which provide the material for much of the *Odyssey*, including the story of the sirens). Yet Socrates' tale is also of a hero: Er, a slain warrior who returns to life on his funeral pyre, able to give an account of the afterlife. This account involves a description of the celestial spheres, arranged in circles on a giant spindle, and 'on the upper surface of each circle is a siren, who goes round with them, hymning a single tone or

---

[3] See ibid., 17 and the references at 39 n2.

note. The eight together form one harmony.'[4] Here the sirens' song is similarly beautiful, but not dangerous – instead its association is with the other side of death, the perfect afterlife in which it represents the harmony of the spheres.

The harmony of the spheres in the Classical world is about the harmonic nature of the movements and proportions between the heavenly bodies in the universe. The sirens who sing this heavenly harmony are representative, not of the enchanting power of an irrationality that leads to a loss of self-control, but of a divine rationality that orders the universe. For us music would be a metaphor, but for the ancients and their medieval inheritors the harmony of the spheres was more than metaphorically music. When, in the sixth century, Anicius Manlius Severinus Boethius's treatise on music theory transmitted much Classical learning about musical tuning and harmonics to the post-classical world, he divided music into three kinds: *musica instrumentalis* (instrumental music, in which he included vocal music, made by the so-called natural instrument of voice); *musica humana* (literally 'human music', but by which he meant not the music that humans make, but the proportions of which they are made up – essentially the harmony of soul and body); and *musica mundana* (celestial music, the music of the spheres). Of these, only one, instrumental music, makes any sound in the sublunary world, so music was not – for the Greeks and the medievals at least – defined by sound, but rather was a feature of rational proportion, which could be (but did not have to be) manifested sonically. In placing the sirens in charge of the celestial music that forms the ultimate expression of this rationality, Plato effectively rescues their song from being irrational and fatal (as it is in the *Odyssey*) and elevates it to a divine harmony, although one that is not audible by those still living on earth.

The harmony of the spheres is at the opposite ethical pole from the song of the sirens in the *Odyssey*, but the two songs share the feature of being irresistibly beautiful. Yet this beauty is, it seems, only good after death; in the world of the living it is potentially deadly unless it is correctly regulated. Odysseus regulated himself by having his crew lash him to the mast; medieval music theory sought instead to regulate music

---

[4] www.davidson.edu/academic/Classics/neumann/CLA350/ErMyth.html.

making: Boethius's music treatise offers a pedagogical understanding of musical tuning – the science of harmonics – that will ensure that *musica instrumentalis* approaches the moral good of the music of the spheres, rather than being the song of the sirens of the sea. Inspired by the greater detail on the harmony of the spheres in Plato's *Timaeus* and other Classical works available to them, several music theorists of the Middle Ages even assigned notes of the scale to the planets in the heavens, mapping the interval series that came between them in diagrammatic forms.[5] In neo-Platonic thought, Music's cosmic proportions, made to sound on earth, speak to the proportions in the human soul and can retune it. If music that is heard retunes the soul, and the soul controls human behaviour, the potential power of musicians is enormous and must be wielded with knowledge and judgement.

Boethius's music treatise influenced hundreds of years of music theory, and the idea of cosmic harmony penetrated deep into the Western musical tradition as a way of arguing against the dangers of the song of the sirens of the sea and in favour of music's divine rationality. In particular its precepts were adopted by those responsible for singing in ecclesiastical contexts, in which the use of music – plainsong – was a central daily practice.

The sound of beauty and Christianity: tension in Augustine

Given their strong Classical legacy, it is unsurprising that early Christian writers both appreciated the power of beautiful sound over the soul and worried about this power's ability to enchant the listener, making him passive and distracted by the beauty of sound – a perilously seductive, feminine form of beauty. In his *Confessions*, written at the very end of the fourth century, Augustine sums this up rather neatly in two contrasting passages. First, he thanks God that

---

[5] The most important other sources were Pliny, Macrobius and Martianus Capella. See Susan Rankin, '*Naturalis concordia vocum cum planetis*: Conceptualizing the Harmony of the Spheres in the Early Middle Ages', in Suzannah Clark and Elizabeth Eva Leach (eds.), *Citation and Authority in Medieval and Renaissance Musical Culture: Learning from the Learned*, Studies in Medieval and Renaissance Music (Woodbridge: Boydell, 2005), 3–19.

he is now cured of his former slavish devotion to the sound of beauty and is focused on the divine words that are sung:

> The delights of the ear drew and held me much more powerfully, but Thou didst unbind and liberate me. In those melodies which Thy words inspire when sung with a sweet and trained voice, I still find repose; yet not so as to cling to them, *but always so as to be able to free myself as I wish.* But it is because of the words which are their life that they gain entry into me and strive for a place of proper honor in my heart; and I can hardly assign them a fitting one.[6]

But he goes straight on to admit that:

> Sometimes, I seem to myself to give them ⌈the melodies⌉ more respect than is fitting, when I see that our minds are more devoutly and earnestly inflamed in piety by the holy words when they are sung than when they are not. And I recognize that all the diverse affections of our spirits have their appropriate measures in the voice and song, to which they are stimulated by I know not what secret correlation. But the pleasures of my flesh – to which the mind ought never to be surrendered nor by them enervated – often beguile me while physical sense does not attend on reason, to follow her patiently, but having once gained entry to help the reason, it strives to run on before her and be her leader. Thus in these things I sin unknowingly, but I come to know it afterward.[7]

---

[6] Augustine, *Confessions*, 10.33.49 (emphasis mine): 'voluptates aurium tenacius me implicaverant et subiugaverant, sed resolvisti et liberasti me. nunc in sonis quos animant eloquia tua cum suavi et artificiosa voce cantantur, fateor, aliquantulum adquiesco, non quidem ut haeream, sed ut surgam cum volo.' www.stoa.org/ hippo/text10.html. Translation by Albert C. Outler, available from www.ccel. org/ccel/augustine/confessions.txt. See Bruce W. Holsinger, *Music, Body, and Desire in Medieval Culture: Hildegard of Bingen to Chaucer*, Figurae: Reading Medieval Culture (Stanford, CA: Stanford University Press, 2001), 69–83.

[7] Augustine, *Confessions*, 10.33.49: 'attamen cum ipsis sententiis, quibus vivunt ut admittantur ad me, quaerunt in corde meo nonnullius dignitatis locum, et vix eis praebeo congruentem. aliquando enim plus mihi videor honoris eis tribuere quam decet, dum ipsis sanctis dictis religiosius et ardentius sentio moveri animos nostros in flammam pietatis cum ita cantantur, quam si non ita cantarentur, et omnes affectus spiritus nostri pro sui diversitate habere proprios modos in voce atque cantu, quorum nescio qua occulta familiaritate excitentur. sed delectatio carnis meae, cui mentem enervandam non oportet dari, saepe me fallit, dum rationi sensus non ita comitatur ut patienter sit posterior, sed tantum, quia propter illam meruit admitti, etiam praecurrere ac ducere conatur. ita in his pecco non sentiens et postea sentio.' www.stoa.org/hippo/text10.html. Translation by Albert C. Outler, available from www.ccel.org/ccel/augustine/confessions.txt.

Led by his senses running ahead of his reason, Augustine worries that the pleasure he takes in hearing liturgical singing in church is a sin of the flesh. A couple of chapters earlier in the *Confessions*, Augustine had already talked about the erotic pull of his past sexual life – before he converted to Christianity – as being something that Christian continence told him to stop his ears against.[8] This stopping of the ears – like the reference to being in the bondage of beautiful sound – seems to be an indirect reference to the story of the sirens itself and reveals that sexual sin and sinful kinds of listening are deeply connected for Augustine. And just as there was one rule for Odysseus and another for his crew, Augustine too recognizes a hierarchy that makes music appropriate for some but not for others, although his hierarchy is tellingly inverted compared to that of the *Odyssey*. Having admitted that he sometime desires the over-extreme austerity of banning singing from the Church entirely, he remembers the tears it caused him to weep when he found his faith originally, and is forced to admit that in terms of its power to convert, singing is useful 'so that by the delights of the ear *the weaker minds* may be stimulated to a devotional mood. Yet when it happens that I am more moved by the singing than by what is sung, I confess myself to have sinned wickedly, and then I would rather not have heard the singing.'[9]

Augustine stresses that reason must lead the senses, not the other way round, and makes it clear that reason lies in what the words of the chant are saying, while the melody appeals to the senses. The idea that music might only be acceptable because it is a vehicle for verbal truths contained in the text is of a piece with the suspicion that the early Church authorities had for untexted music, which was typically used for dancing. In such cases, the lack of a text whose higher and rational truths might excuse the pleasure taken by hearers of the melody was compounded by

---

[8] See Judith Ann Peraino, *Listening to the Sirens: Musical Technologies of Queer Identity from Homer to Hedwig* (Berkeley and London: University of California Press, 2005), 39.

[9] Augustine, *Confessions*, 10.33.49 (emphasis mine): 'ut per oblectamenta aurium infirmior animus in affectum pietatis adsurgat. tamen cum mihi accidit ut me amplius cantus quam res quae canitur moveat, poenaliter me peccare confiteor et tunc mallem non audire cantantem.' www.stoa.org/hippo/text10.html. Translation by Albert C. Outler, available from www.ccel.org/ccel/augustine/confessions.txt.

the purpose of the wordless music, which was designed to animate bodies through dancing – a social, physical and sensual practice that offered sinful opportunities for participants and spectators alike.

Elsewhere in his writings, however, Augustine talks more positively about the musical element of singing when he talks of the 'jubilus' – by which he seems to mean the melisma on the final syllable of the chant setting the words 'alleluia'. This melisma typically consisted of many notes that simply prolong the sounding of the final syllable in time rather than setting any new text. The 'Alleluia' as a whole is not entirely without text, but the long melisma at the end is so much an extension of a single syllable of text that rather than conveying the sense of the word itself it instead gives expression to a pure emotion. As Augustine says:

> One who jubilates does not speak words, but it is rather a sort of sound of joy without words; for the voice of the soul is poured out in joy, showing as much as it is able the feeling without comprehending the sense. A man joying in his exultation, from certain unspeakable and incomprehensible words, bursts forth in a certain voice of exultations without words, so that it seems he does indeed rejoice with his own voice, but as if, because filled with too much joy, he cannot put into words what it is in which he delights.[10]

The sound of the heart rejoicing without words is acceptable to Augustine not only because it rejoices in the praise of God, but also because Augustine speaks of the performer's perspective. Augustine accepts the musical expression of joy as a performer because one can regulate the sound and know its pure intention when one is actually generating it. Conversely, when one is merely a passive listener, the effect is altogether different: the listener must be able to assess the rational content of the sound, its sacred words and the good intention of the performer in producing it without being carried away by rapturous – irrational and dangerous – enjoyment of the sound itself. Rarely, however, is there a singer without a listener, and even when everyone present is singing, they are also all listening. The danger of being charmed by one's own voice, hinted at in Augustine's writing, remains as a troublingly autoerotic possibility.

[10] Holsinger, *Music, Body, and Desire*, 76.

Positive containment 1: the pedagogical rationalization of chant

For those like Augustine who saw the value and beauty in music but worried about its potential to distract from the contemplation of moral good, it was necessary to emphasize the rational and ethical aspects of music. In his music treatise Boethius, summarizing Plato's strictures in the *Republic*, defines music of the highest character as 'temperate, simple, and masculine [*modesta, simplex, mascula*]', rather than 'effeminate, violent, or fickle [*effeminata, fera, varia*]'.[11] These binaries are repeated verbatim by a vast array of subsequent theorists.[12] In terms of medieval rhetorical tropes which insisted that gender categories were biologically determined and immutable, producing good music meant de-emphasizing passive appreciation of music's beauty as something feminine, seductive, de-rationalizing, effeminizing, in favour of an active engagement with music's rationality as something masculine, numerical, quantifiable, and part of the active mental engagement of a performer. This was especially the case in the Christian Middle Ages when the sung liturgy of the Church was central to the everyday praise of God – banning music in church was just not an option. To ensure that it was the right kind of music, the teaching and study of music – the discipline of *musica* – developed a specific pedagogy in which the very definition of what was and what was not music was based on music's expression of a rationality that belongs only to humans and not to other animals. Most typically in theoretical and pedagogical contexts, this rationality expressed itself in the ability to understand the mathematical ratios that underlie the correct tuning of musical intervals with the range of notes used in chant.

However, for most writers of this period even tuned sounds – whose intervals exhibit such ratios – merit the status of music only when they are both produced and received by an intellectually engaged rational

---

[11] Anicius Manlius Severinus Boethius, *Fundamentals of Music*, ed. Claude V. Palisca, trans. Calvin M. Bower, Music Theory Translation (New Haven and London: Yale University Press, 1989), 3.

[12] See Elizabeth Eva Leach, 'Gendering the Semitone, Sexing the Leading Tone: Fourteenth-Century Music Theory and the Directed Progression', *Music Theory Spectrum*, 28/1 (2006), 1–21; Elizabeth Eva Leach, 'Music and Masculinity in the Middle Ages', in Ian Biddle and Kirsten Gibson (eds.), *Masculinity and Western Musical Practice* (Farnham: Ashgate, 2009), 21–39.

animal. Again, this thinking is carried over from earlier antique understandings of music. Even before he converted to Christianity, Augustine started writing a music treatise cast in the form of a dialogue between a master and a pupil. In stressing to the pupil that *musica* is a science – that is, something involving knowledge – the master uses the example of the song of the nightingale.

> MASTER: Tell me, then, whether the nightingale seems to make proper
> intervals with its voice well in the spring of the year. For its song
> is both harmonious, and sweet and, unless I'm mistaken, it fits
> the season.
> PUPIL: It seems quite so.
> M. But it isn't trained in the liberal discipline, is it?
> P. No.
> M. You see, then, the noun 'science' is indispensable to the definition.
> P. I see it clearly.
> M. Now tell me, then, don't they all seem to be a kind with the
> nightingale, all those which sing under the guidance of a certain sense,
> that is, do it harmoniously and sweetly, although if they were
> questioned about these number or intervals of high and low notes they
> could not reply?
> P. I think they are very much alike.
> M. And what's more, aren't those who like to listen to them without this
> science to be compared to beasts? For we see elephants, bears,
> and many other kinds of beasts are moved by singing, and birds
> themselves are charmed by their own voices. For, with no further
> proper purpose, they would not do this with such effort without
> some pleasure.[13]

So the pupil agrees that the voice of the nightingale *sounds* like music, but when it is pointed out to him that the bird is not trained in *musica* – the liberal discipline of music, which makes music the rational property of humans – he admits that birdsong should not really be considered as

---

[13] Translation Saint Augustine, 'On Music', trans. Robert Catesby Taliaferro, in Robert Catesby Taliaferro (ed.), *Writings of Saint Augustine, Volume 2*, The Fathers of the Church: A New Translation 4 (Washington, D.C.: Catholic University of America Press in association with Consortium Books, 1977), 151–379, 176–7 adapted (I have replaced 'mensurate' with 'make proper intervals with'). Latin available at www.chmtl.indiana.edu/tml/3rd-5th/AUGDEM1_TEXT.html.

music in that strict sense. The master then extrapolates to liken the nightingale's lovely but irrational non-music to the playing of human performers guided only by a certain sense but lacking the understanding of their own practice. And he goes further: people who like to listen to such non-music without themselves understanding the rationality – the science – that makes music *music* can be compared to the elephants, bears and many other kinds of beasts that are moved by singing.[14] The mere enjoyment of beautiful sound doesn't make the listener human; nor does it make that sound music, which is seen as being by definition something human.

Augustine again outlines many of the issues that extend throughout the Middle Ages. He demands that even if the song sounds sweet and well measured, the musicians must know what they are doing or they are no better than animals; and listeners who take pleasure in music by musicians who do not know what they are doing are also no better than beasts. That which makes music a science or an art is that which separates it from nature and from the natural voices of birds and other animals that *seem* to sing. The performer of music is under an obligation, not just to make musical sounds, but to understand them as *musica*, that is, as proportions that are rational. The listener is also under an obligation to understand sounds in this way, whether or not their performing agent does so. Whether that performer is a bird or an unthinking human, by listening actively the medieval hearer, who can tell whether or not the beautiful sound is music or not, can avoid being reduced to a similarly bestial status.

The problem for music pedagogy, however, was that it was reliant on models taken from the teaching of language.[15] It was relatively easy for medieval grammarians to differentiate language from non-linguistic utterance, because language conveys semantic content with its sound (or, as medieval grammarians said, its *vox* has *verbum*). The rational content of language is thus semantic, binding it tightly to human agents wanting to communicate sensible information. But the rational

---

[14] Ibid., 176–7.
[15] See Elizabeth Eva Leach, 'Grammar in the Medieval Song-School', *New Medieval Literatures*, 11 (2009), 195–211.

component of music is its ratios – the tuning of its sounds – which is something that species other than humans use to communicate in a distinctly non-linguistic manner. So music's ontology could not readily be pinned down using grammatical models: music-like intervals could be imitated by birds or untrained singers with a good ear so that a listener could never be sure that the seemingly rational sound being heard was not something dangerously irrational. Given that medieval authorities viewed women as less rational than men, we might now begin to appreciate why in their earliest instantiations, the sirens are hybrids of women and birds.[16]

Many later clerical writers took their cue from Augustine's ambivalence about listening to music and sought to impose strictures on what they viewed as feminine and feminizing excesses in performance. The twelfth-century writer John of Salisbury, for example, criticizes those singing in church services for what he identifies as the 'lightness and dissolution of dainty voices designed to achieve vainglory in the feminine manner'.[17] 'Thou wouldst think', John continues, 'that these were the most delicious songs of very pleasing sirens – not of men – and thou wouldst marvel at the lightness of voice, which cannot be compared in all their measures and pleasing melodies to those of the nightingale or parrot, or any other more clear-sounding bird that might be found.'[18] These male singers' effeminacy and effeminizing powers are stronger and all the more worrisome on account of their virtuosity. John describes the singers as *more* eloquent than two natural avian practitioners but says that their sound would make a listener mistake them for sirens – women–bird hybrids – rather than men.[19] Rationality is the defining feature, not only of the human soul, but specifically of both masculinity and *musica*,

[16] See Elizabeth Eva Leach, *Sung Birds: Music, Nature, and Poetry in the Later Middle Ages* (Ithaca: Cornell University Press, 2007), chapter 5 and Elizabeth Eva Leach, '"The Little Pipe Sings Sweetly While the Fowler Deceives the Bird": Sirens in the Later Middle Ages', *Music and Letters*, 87/2 (2006), 187–211.

[17] See K. S. B. Keats-Rohan (ed.), *Ioannis Sarisburiensis Policraticus I–IV*, Corpus Christianorum Continuatio mediaeualis 118 (Turnhout: Brepols, 1993), 1.6 (pages 48–9) and the discussion in Leach, '"The Little Pipe Sings Sweetly While the Fowler Deceives the Bird"', 188–9 and Leach, *Sung Birds*, 203–9.

[18] See Keats-Rohan (ed.), *Ioannis Sarisburiensis Policraticus I–IV*, 1.6; Leach, '"The Little Pipe Sings Sweetly While the Fowler Deceives the Bird"', 188–9; Leach, *Sung Birds*, 153.

[19] See Leach, '"The Little Pipe Sings Sweetly While the Fowler Deceives the Bird"'.

differentiating men both from beasts (including birds) and from women. According to John of Salisbury, the beautiful sound of accomplished singers take the singers – and potentially their passive listeners – away from their humanity and their masculinity, making them effeminate, monstrous, unnatural.

Sirens appear in medieval bestiaries, where – like all bestiary animals – they are explained as encoding a moral message.[20] Medieval moralizations of the sirens mention their singing and the danger it poses, explaining it in terms of various worldly blandishments: money, rich food, illegitimate sex, and other sensory excesses. Manuscript illuminations for this particular beast typically depict three sirens as a visual embodiment of Boethius's three species of *musica instrumentalis*: one plucks a stringed instrument, one plays a wind instrument and the third sings (see Figure 4.1). As in Figure 4.1, where a man is being physically torn in two as he hears the sirens' music, sirens served as a convenient reminder that sonic beauty could be dangerous. Sometimes sirens turn up visually in churches, sculpted on corbels or decorating the exterior masonry, or inked into books designed for use in church services.[21] Reading these images required a certain amount of decoding from the viewer, and thus poses complex questions of interpretation for us. Figure 4.2 shows a page from a late thirteenth-century chant book, possibly from England but now in France, on which a bird-footed, winged siren stands holding up the cadential formula that will connect the 'in secula seculorum' at the end of the chant back to the repeat of an earlier bit of the chant.

What does this mean? Is it a warning? Or a joke? It is perhaps significant that the siren occurs in the chants for the Office for St Cecilia – a woman whose link to music was very clear but whose moral propriety – and especially her sexual continence – was even clearer: her legend tells. that at her wedding she sat away from the other guests, singing psalms, and thereafter managed to keep her husband from her bed and convert him to Christianity, thereby remaining a virgin. The siren who supports

---

[20] See ibid.

[21] See Jacqueline Leclercq-Marx, *La Sirène dans la pensée et dans l'art de l'Antiquité et du Moyen Âge: du mythe païen au symbol chrétien* (Brussels: Academie Royale de Belgique, 1997); Anthony Weir and Jim Jerman, *Images of Lust: Sexual Carvings on Medieval Churches* (London: Batsford, 1986; repr. London: Routledge, 1999).

FIGURE 4.1. Nude sirens in a Bestiary. Oxford, Bodleian Library MS Bodley 602, f.10r. Image courtesy of the Bodleian Library, University of Oxford.

FIGURE 4.2. Helpful siren in the Office for St Cecilia. Vendôme, Bibliothèque Municipale 0017E, f. 527v. Image © Institut de recherche et d'histoire des textes – CNRS.

part of St Cecilia's office acts as a counterpoise to Cecilia's musical virginity as a reminder of the ever-lurking presence of musical – and moral – impropriety. Both of music's ethical possibilities are brought plainly into view in the hope, perhaps, that only one is translated into sound.

Positive containment 2: vicarious courtly pleasures

Outside the cloister, practitioners pursued slightly different methods of shoring up music's ethical goodness to enable the appreciation of beautiful sounds in despite of their detractors. Even dance music – melody with or without words for people to move their bodies to – had its apologists. Because it was not associated with the literate musicians of the cloister or court chapels, instrumental music was rarely written down in the Middle Ages. One of the earliest discussions from Western Europe was written around 1300 by a Norman music theorist called Johannes de Grocheio. His discussion of the musical practices of late thirteenth-century Paris describes a number of instrumental genres and dance forms.[22] Grocheio, who was influenced by the new Aristotelian philosophy of the late medieval universities – which had far more time for music than its more Platonic forerunner – tries to validate much-criticized secular musical forms. Specifically he claims that music diverts young minds away from vice, and away from sexual vice in particular. A genre he calls the *cantus coronatus* has inherent *bonitas* – goodness – in it; the *cantus versualis*, while not on the same level, should nevertheless be 'performed for the young

---

[22] Edition and translation Christopher Page, 'Johannes Grocheio on Secular Music: A Corrected Text and a New Translation', *Plainsong and Medieval Music*, 2 (1993), 17–41, 31–2. Earlier edition of the Latin text of Grocheio's treatise is available in open source at www.chmtl.indiana.edu/tml/14th/GRODEM_TEXT.html. See also Lawrence Gushee, 'Questions of Genre in Medieval Treatises on Music', in Wulf Arlt, Ernst Lichtenhahn and Hans Oesch (eds.), *Gattungen der Musik in Einzeldarstellungen: Gedenkschrift Leo Schrade* (Bern: Francke, 1973), 365–433, 386. The *ductia* is also 'cum decenti percussione mensuratus,' which Page translates as 'with an appropriate beat' and Gushee as 'measured by seemly percussion'. Grocheio has, however, just cited Aristotle as authority to the fact that although instrumental sounds are commonly subdivided by the means of production into those produced by blowing or by striking, all sound is ultimately the result of percussion. Grocheio's 'cum decenti percussione mensuratus' (with properly measured striking) may thus mean that it is discretely pitched (since measure more often pertains to pitch than the 'beat' of Page's interpretation) or merely 'correctly produced'.

Elizabeth Eva Leach

lest they be found ever in idleness'. This is the same reason that the sung dance form called the *stantipes* is praised – because it represents, in the diversity of its rhymes and music, a level of difficulty that 'makes the minds of young men and of girls dwell upon this, and leads them away from depraved thoughts'. The nature of these depraved thoughts is elucidated more explicitly in the genre Grocheio calls the *ductia*, whose name he derives from the explanation that it leads the hearts (*ducit corda*) of young people away from vain thoughts 'and is said to have power against that passion which is called "erotic love"'.[23]

The *ductia* forms the instrumental accompaniment to the *carole*, a kind of dance, in which men and women typically held hands in a circle or a line and which unsurprisingly was frequently condemned by preachers in the later Middle Ages. One sermon story, designed to put people off such dances, concerns a flute player who urges youths and maidens to dance to songs that inspire obscene and vulgar thoughts and behaviour. As the flautist tarries in the street at vespers, he is struck dead by lightning. And when his corpse is buried in holy ground, its grave is robbed by a number of devils who turn up in the middle of the night to carry his body off to where it truly belongs.[24] Grocheio's writings counter this widespread religious opposition specifically to claim that such dance songs distract the young from precisely the same emotions that the preachers maintain they inspire.

The most famous French poet and composer of the fourteenth century, Guillaume de Machaut (*c.* 1300–77), similarly stresses music's power to inspire joy of a very moral kind. In the *Prologue* to his collected works, the poet notes that spending time composing songs causes happiness, gaiety and joy because no one intent on such things quarrels or argues or thinks of immorality, hate, foolishness or scandal. Composition requires concentration on its own process and thus precludes other thoughts.

> Car quant je sui en ce penser,
> Je ne porroie a riens penser
> Fors que seulement au propos

[23] Page, 'Johannes Grocheio on Secular Music', 23–4; 26–7.
[24] R. F. Bennett, *The Early Dominicans: Studies in Thirteenth-Century Dominican History* (Cambridge: Cambridge University Press, 1937), 119.

Dont faire dit ou chant propos;
Et s'a autre chose pensoie,
Toute mon ouevre defferoie.
(For when I am so minded [as to write poetry or song], I wouldn't be able
    to think about anything except this sole purpose of making the proposed
    poem or song; and if I were to think of something else, I would
    completely undo all my work.)[25]

Here we have the idea that composition not only keeps despair at bay, but
also – like dancing the *ductia* – avoids creating idle hands for which the
devil might find work.[26]

As seen in Augustine's comments above, a positive moral aspect is
available for those making music, whether through performance or composition, but Machaut's larger output – a mixture of narrative poems,
lyrics and music – propounds a similarly moral role for music for its
listeners in the very distinctly non-pedagogical ambience of the court. His
audience are not necessarily trained musicians; they do not necessarily
know about *musica*, but they do know about moral good, about beauty,
and about different kinds of love – and their good and bad effects.
Machaut's poetry and music taught his lay audience about the importance
of hope, often personified for the didactic purpose as the noble Lady
Hope.[27] As courtiers living in a mixed-sex community, their spiritual,
existential, and practical needs were rather different from those of regular
monks who could see music as reflecting divine neo-Platonic harmonies.
Instead, lay persons – essentially later versions of those 'weaker spirits'
that Augustine mentioned – could use beautiful sound as a pleasurable
form of ethical education. Practically, a beautiful song inscribes itself in
memory with its text, making Machaut's short lyric items very memor-
able. As Machaut's lyrics often summarize and epitomize ethical issues
discussed at greater length in his narrative poems, his songs effectively
served as a short-cut aide-memoire for his ethical programme. Most
importantly, the pleasure of listening to a beautiful song acts as a

---

[25] Ernest Hoepffner, *Oeuvres de Guillaume de Machaut*, 3 vols. (Paris: Firmin-Didot,
    1908–22), 1:7, V, ll.37–42.
[26] See Elizabeth Eva Leach, *Guillaume de Machaut: Secretary, Poet, Musician* (Ithaca:
    Cornell University Press, 2011), chapter 3.
[27] See ibid., chapter 4.

stand-in for the pleasures that the song might describe. In some cases the song depicts the pleasure of hunting, replicating the sounds of the chase and giving a vicarious pleasure that takes up far less time than a real hunt would.[28] But courtly song more typically celebrates – and replaces – a more amorous chase: the pursuit of ladies. Machaut's balade with the apt incipit 'Beauty' (*Biauté* (B4); see Figure 4.3) describes a peerless lady, of refined sweetness, with a body worthy of all praise, a soft face, beautiful glance, and a joyful appearance. Unfortunately for the lover, this beauty, too, is deadly – the lack of encouragement that he gets from her has brought him to the point of death.[29] But the music of the song has its own beauties, both auditory and – in this case – visual.

The notation is beautified by the use of red colouration (it is no coincidence that the words for red and beauty are related in many languages); and the sound of the melisma where the red colouration is, which terminates the three main sections of each stanza of the song, is a lovely musical sequence, replete with plangent dissonances and a wonderfully undulating contour. Like the melisma of the *jubilus* of the Alleluia mentioned by Augustine, this melisma enables the singer to 'just sing', and conveys to the listener wordless emotion. The listener to this song gains aural and visual representations of the lady's beauty and of the lover's pain, and the time spent listening to the song at once distracts and consoles.[30]

The promotion of musical items, especially songs, as objects of visual as well as auditory beauty was taken to a high level in the court cultures of the later fourteenth and fifteenth centuries. Individual songs exist in

---

[28] See the analysis of the depiction of a hunt in Denis le Grant's *Se je chant* in Leach, *Sung Birds*, chapter 4.

[29] See the lengthier analysis in Elizabeth Eva Leach, 'Death of a Lover and the Birth of the Polyphonic Balade: Machaut's Notated Balades 1–5', *Journal of Musicology*, 19/3 (2002), 461–502, 488–92.

[30] I recommend in particular the recording by the Ferrara Ensemble, which is performed in the original two-part arrangement. On music and consolation in Machaut see Leach, *Guillaume de Machaut*, chapters 4–6; Elizabeth Eva Leach, 'Poet as Musician', in Deborah McGrady and Jennifer Bain (eds.), *A Companion to Guillaume de Machaut* (Leiden: Brill, 2012), 49–66; and Sarah Kay, 'Touching Singularity: Consolation, Philosophy, and Poetry in the French *dit*', in Catherine E. Léglu and Stephen J. Milner (eds.), *The Erotics of Consolation: Desire and Distance in the Late Middle Ages*, The New Middle Ages (Basingstoke and New York: Palgrave Macmillan, 2008), 21–38.

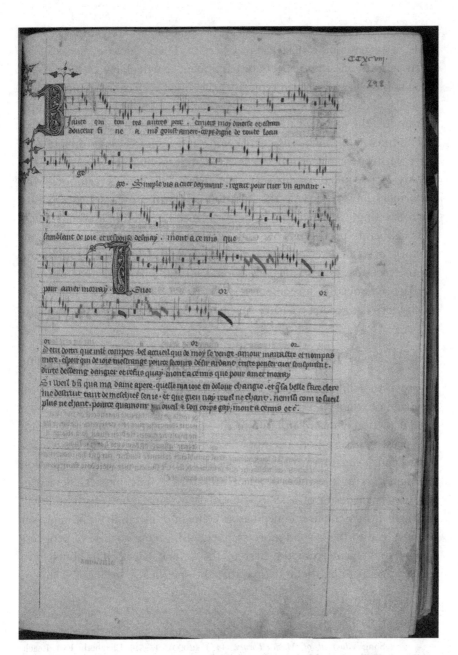

FIGURE 4.3. Guillaume de Machaut's balade *Biauté* (B4). The Ferrell-Vogüé MS, f.298r. On loan to the Parker Library, Corpus Christi, Cambridge. Reproduced by kind permission of Elizabeth J. and James E. Ferrell. Colour image available on the DIAMM website.

manuscript copies with the musical staves shaped variously into a heart, a circle, a seven-course maze, and a harp.[31] These 'picture pieces' were given as gifts on single sheets of parchment, particularly at New Year, when noblemen and women typically exchanged very costly items. One of these, Jacob Senleches's *La harpe de melodie* (see Figure 4.4), sets a text that invites the recipient to see and hear the notes of the melodious harp.

The music to which this text is sung is presented on an image of a harp, with notes placed on the harp strings giving the pitches of the melody. A red-inked rondeau wrapped around the harp's frame tells the performers how to decode the notation, which represents two separate parts as a single written part to be performed in canon (a kind of round). This deliberate prettifying of song, turning it into a beautiful object, an artwork, even an artefact, serves to make beautiful song into a surrogate for the pleasure it describes, a safe and ethical surrogate that must be experienced socially, in company, and gives a pleasure that is not the much more dangerous pleasure that is sought by the desire for the lady.

Desire for music and the music of desire: back to the sirens

In order to fulfil such kinds of function more effectively, the musical language of what we now call the later Middle Ages developed its own aural depiction of desire and fulfilment – or expectation and achievement. The present description attempts discussion in fairly unspecialized language; musically literate readers seeking a more technical explanation will find this in the musicological literature.[32] The musical device in question is made up of a succession of two sonic moments that I will here call chords: the first chord has an element of instability that makes it seem to lead to the second more stable chord, giving a sense of progression or movement from the first to the second chord. The fourteenth century seems to be the first time that the specifically harmonic element

---

[31] Reproductions of all four 'picture pieces' can be found in Leach, *Sung Birds*, chapter 3.

[32] See Elizabeth Eva Leach, 'Counterpoint and Analysis in Fourteenth-Century Song', *Journal of Music Theory*, 44/1 (2000), 45–79; Elizabeth Eva Leach, 'Guillaume de Machaut's *De petit po* (B18)', in Michael Tenzer and John Roeder (eds.), *Analytical and Cross-Cultural Studies in World Music* (Oxford: Oxford University Press, 2012), 56–97.

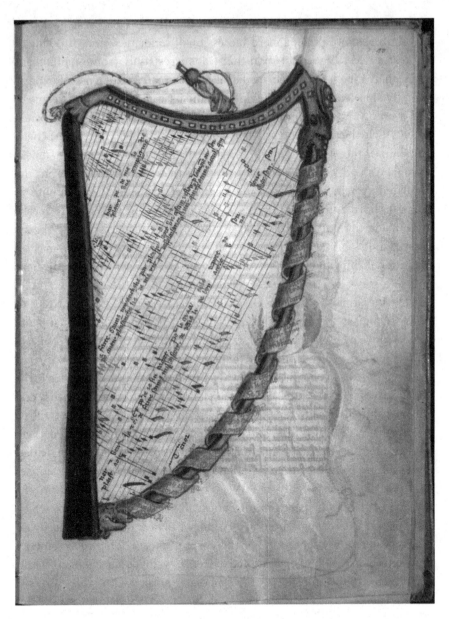

FIGURE 4.4. Jacob Senleches, *La harpe de melodie*. Chicago, Newberry Library 54.1, f.10r. Photo courtesy of the Newberry Library, Chicago.

of music was able to figure expectation aurally.[33] This presentation of two chords is more than a mere succession of sonorities, since it is able to suggest a necessary connection that leads irresistibly from one moment to another. Like later music, medieval music creates that sense of expectation by sharpening one of the notes in the first chord so that it seems to lead a note very close in pitch to it in the second chord. This sharpened note, which there is evidence that singers might have 'over-sharpened', destabilized the overall sonority, making the first chord teeter into a near dissonance, and led very strongly towards the note of resolution. In the regulated system of medieval *musica*, the note causing the instability in the first chord and prompting the sense of movement was strictly speaking outside the normal collection of pitches that medieval music theory described: it loosened the pedagogical rope binding music to the mast of the rational ship; and it did so while making the listener long for the next note of a song.

This adjustment of the notes was 'for reasons of beauty' according to medieval music theorists, who distinguished it from pitch adjustments made 'for reasons of necessity', which was just a rule about properly tuning certain 'perfect intervals' (octaves, fifths, and unisons) to prevent really harsh dissonances. So, it was completely necessary to tune the perfectly consonant and highly stable intervals of octaves, fifths, and unisons; but inflecting the tuning of the imperfectly consonant thirds and sixths was beautiful – and was something that destabilized them further, creating the aural image of a temporal progression of sonorities, one resulting from the other. The action of sharpening the leading note of the first chord, especially if it was 'over-sharpened', resulted in the division of the pitch spectrum into unusually small interval steps, which were placed where small intervals within the octave did not ordinarily go in the system known as *musica recta* (correct music). This represented a double transgression of the rational system developed for chant so that it could reflect the music of the spheres; music with this directed

---

[33] See Richard L. Crocker, 'Discant, Counterpoint and Harmony', *Journal of the American Musicological Society*, 15 (1962), 1–21; Sarah Fuller, 'Tendencies and Resolutions: The Directed Progression in *Ars Nova* Music', *Journal of Music Theory*, 36/2 (1992), 229–57; David Maw, 'Redemption and Retrospection in Jacques of Liège's Concept of *Cadentia*', *Early Music History*, 29 (2010), 79–118.

progression was very worldly music indeed. In the mid-fourteenth century the music theorist Johannes Boen notes that young men, sick of the regular diatonic gamut, 'admit more notes than the ancients because they pursue, mouths agape, the wantonness of the song itself [*lasciviam ipsius cantus*]'.[34] The use of the word 'lascivia' – from which we get the English 'lasciviousness' – to describe this open-mouthed longing for new notes already starts to admit an interpretation of this kind of listening as a potentially dangerous kind of aural erotics. Another theorist from the period, Arnulf, also uses this word as he notes among the most able kind of singers

> a second group – that is to say of the favoured female sex – which is so much the more precious the more it is rare; when she freely divides tones into semitones with a sweet-sounding throat, and divides semitones into indivisible microtones [*athomos*], she enjoys herself [*lascivit*] with an indescribable melody that you would rather deem angelic than human.[35]

Unsurprisingly the theorist then goes on to liken these women to 'earthly Sirens' who

> enchant the bewitched ears of their listeners and they steal away their hearts, which are for the most part lulled by this kind of intoxication, in secret theft, and having snatched them and made them subject to their will, they then enslave them and lead them, shipwrecked by the beauty, alas!, of their prison, into an earthly Charybdis in which no kind of redemption or ransom is available.[36]

This writer seems specifically to link the singing of small intervals – the atoms of pitch – with the beauty of these singers' song. But then he goes on to note the dangers of the song, causing the soporific intoxication of

---

[34] Translation by Leofranc Holford-Strevens. See Leach, 'Gendering the Semitone', 12–13. Open source edition of the Latin text can be found at www.chmtl.indiana.edu/tml/14th/BOENMUS_TEXT.html.

[35] Translation adapted from that in Christopher Page, 'A Treatise on Musicians from ?c.1400: The *Tractatulus de differentiis et gradibus cantorum*', *Journal of the Royal Musical Association*, 117 (1992), 1–21, 20, which gives the Latin on 17. Open source for the Latin can be found at www.chmtl.indiana.edu/tml/14th/ARNTRA_TEXT.html.

[36] For further comments, see Leach, '"The Little Pipe Sings Sweetly While the Fowler Deceives the Bird"', and *Sung Birds*, chapter 5. This translation from Page, 'A Treatise on Musicians from ?c.1400', 20, Latin on 17.

its listeners who love their subjection to the beauty of the prison as an earthly Charybdis from which there is no escape.

Arnulf's text testifies to the already-mentioned underlying problem of the beauty of sound – the problem of the feminine. Music's link to femininity – or, at the very least, its ability to undermine typical Western constructions of self-willed, active masculinity by making listeners passive, soporific and *subject* to the musical sound – seems to be at the root of the problem with the sound of beauty. These problems continue to beset music throughout its history, from the Greeks to the present day, never winning the day, but always providing ammunition for those who found their own or others' subjection to beautiful sound distasteful – who resented having their own emotions manipulated by a mere singer or player, or – more latterly – by the disembodied sounds of electronic reproduction. And authorities continued to worry about the sirens: later tonal music in the West famously extended the two-chord sequence that controlled time aurally, figuring desire and resolution, to enormous temporal proportions in the music of the nineteenth century. It is possible to understand the entire four hours of Wagner's opera *Tristan and Isolde*, for example, as being animated tonally by repeated non-resolving presentations of the first chord of this tension–resolution sequence, ornamentally extended (music analysts would say 'prolonged') throughout the entire opera, resolving only at the end.[37] Such an analysis might explain – at least in part – why a 1992 report into church music, commissioned by the Archbishops of Canterbury and York, specifically condemned the music of Wagner.[38] The sound of beauty is dangerous.

Narratives responding to the sound of beauty have throughout history see-sawed between condemning it as the song of the sirens of the sea and lauding it as the music of more heavenly sirens. If the voices of warning predominate at particular periods it is largely because the educated elites who voice such warnings are more likely to leave written records of their criticisms, while those who have no such moral qualms are more likely to

---

[37] For a fuller exposition see Richard Taruskin, *Music in the Nineteenth Century*, The Oxford History of Western Music, vol. III (2nd edn 2010; New York: Oxford University Press, 2005), 539–57.

[38] See *In Tune with Heaven: The Report of the Archbishops' Commission on Church Music* (London: Church House Publishing and Hodder & Stoughton, 1992), 35.

be enjoying themselves playing, singing, and dancing. In all periods it is possible to find those who extolled the joyful beauty of music, those who warned that a moral kind of sonic beauty was only assured within the correct regulatory framework, and those for whom most or nearly all music was simply immoral. In the nineteenth century the apologists for music tried to downgrade the problematic category of beauty – effectively accepting from its detractors that anything beautiful was feminine and ornamental – and adopted as their own category for positive beauty the idea of the sublime.[39] The sublime enabled its listeners to evade charges of feminine seduction for a much more reassuringly masculine, awesome, even terrifying kind of aural pleasure. The elevation of difficult music – and ultimately, in the so-called postmodern sublime of the twentieth century, of music that seemed to espouse a deliberate ugliness – seemed responsibly and ethically to reflect the terrifying horrors of modernity and at once confirmed the negative judgements of beautiful sounds' detractors while opening up a space in which deep aesthetic responses – even passive subjection – to music could still be justified.[40]

Conclusion

The sound of beauty can serve as a sonic manifestation of a moral good, of the divine, of the music of the spheres, a glimpse into the mind of God. Like most forms of beauty, however, it can also serve a negative purpose, distracting and seducing, especially when corrupted by the venal mouths of human singers or divorced from a guiding text in wordless melismas or instrumental music. Like Odysseus bound to the mast, wise men in the past sought to constrain their own musical practices by emphasizing music's rational content, tying it tightly to good words, and insisting that its practice was strictly regulated. But music was too subtle, too beautiful, too irrational and irregular. The masculine sublime of modern

---

[39] See, for example, the discussion of the symphony in Mark Evan Bonds, *Music as Thought: Listening to the Symphony in the Age of Beethoven* (Princeton: Princeton University Press, 2006).
[40] For a discussion, which ultimately rejects a strong distinction between romantic and postmodern sublime but places music centrally, see Kiene Brillenburg Wurth, *Musically Sublime: Indeterminacy, Infinity, Irresolvability* (New York: Fordham University Press, 2009).

music (by which I mean music after around 1800) and the masculine rationality of earlier musical pedagogy are both attempts to remain in control while ceding control. After all, Odysseus managed this: he set up the control of himself by having himself tied to the masts and cautioning the sailors to ignore any countermand while the sirens were singing. He was thus able to subject himself safely to beautiful sound, without becoming enslaved to it.

The debates about the sound of beauty indicate clearly the cultural importance of music, and why it has been and remains something over which people argue, legislate and worry. Fundamentally they bring us up against the compound nature of the human, the intersection of what Aristotle would call the animal soul and the rational soul, promising us something that only a rational human can attain but ultimately showing us that we are also just animals. Whatever the music in question, its ability to merge the immiscible elements of being human makes it resemble nothing so much as human Being itself.[41]

---

[41] The idea of musical structure as mimetic of human Being, an account fusing Heideggerian and Schenkerian ideas, can be found in J. P. E. Harper-Scott, *Edward Elgar, Modernist* (Cambridge: Cambridge University Press, 2006).

5 Beauty and attraction: in the 'eye' of the beholder

JEANNE ALTMANN

> Beauty in things exists merely in the mind which contemplates them.
> David Hume, *Essays, Moral and Political* (1742)

Envision some visitors who have travelled to Kenya to observe wildlife (Figure 5.1A). They first encounter a pair of baboons mating. The visitor group quickly drives away muttering, perhaps after covering their children's eyes. Coming upon a ranger or a field scientist, the parents splutter their outrage at such an X-rated sight. A pair of mating lions or elephants is encountered next; cameras roll, and if a tour guide is present he is given an extra tip for such a wonderful sighting. A male baboon kills and feeds on prey, perhaps a gazelle; the visitors recoil, and may even seek a wildlife ranger to complain about the horrible scene that they have witnessed: can't somebody stop the baboons from doing this terrible thing (see Figure 5.1B)? A lion kills and feeds on prey, perhaps a gazelle, wildebeest or baboon; again cameras roll, and more visitors are attracted to the awesome sight, delighted to have witnessed one of the highlights of anyone's African safari. These scenarios or slight variations on them occur frequently in African wildlife reserves.

What diverse responses there are to similar behaviour exhibited by three mammal species, each large, group-living and highly social! When and why are humans variously repulsed, nonplussed, or attracted to ostensibly similar events? Why is sexual or predatory behaviour by lions but not by baboons attractive to many people? The answer seems to lie primarily in our obvious similarity to baboons, more similar than to lions and to elephants, and perhaps the consequent embarrassment that comes from watching behaviour that would not be comfortable to watch if it were people performing. This kind of differential response to various

Jeanne Altmann

FIGURE 5.1. Depending on the species being observed, people often
have different reactions to viewing ostensibly similar behaviour such as mating (5.1A)
or predation (5.1B), and find these behaviours attractive when observed in some species,
such as lions, and disturbing or even repulsive in others, such as baboons. Image of
mating elephants courtesy of Peter Granli; other images by author.

species is familiar to conservation biologists, who regularly deal with people's differential willingness to work for the survival of some species versus others; large, furry, round-faced and large-eyed mammals are particularly appealing. Outside the conservation community, however, relatively little attention is paid to these biased responses. A more nuanced study of attraction and repulsion would reveal subtle characteristics and provide insights into our understanding of how our emotions contribute to our views on a wide range of topics. The relatively new field of Conservation Psychology explores such questions.

A second example of differential human perception of beauty or attraction can be seen in the reactions of *different* people to the *same* species, specifically visual depictions of baboons by two artists (Figure 5.2).

The painter Deborah Ross has spent many years in rural areas of Africa as a wildlife artist and art instructor for children and adults. Most artists whose subjects are African wildlife – and there are many – focus primarily on elephants, rhinoceros, buffalo, giraffe, great apes, and large carnivores. They simply ignore baboons. Ross, by contrast, not only is attracted to baboons as subjects, but depicts them in a way very different from that of the unidentified artist in the advertisement for a film shown in Figure 5.2. You would hardly know it was the same species being depicted by the two artists, and this is the case not just for the poses of individual baboons, but also for the depiction of baboon society, as can be seen in the depictions of attacking hordes versus peaceful foraging groups. The different depictions are further reinforced by the use of bold and stark colours with strong lines versus watercolours in muted tones. It is astonishing how much people's reactions can differ in response to similar physical traits and behaviours.

What is shared and what differs among members of a species in their attractions, what we might call their sense of beauty? To what extent do individuals' different backgrounds, experiences and sensory abilities affect their attractions? We take our own human, cultural and individual perspective so much for granted that we often have difficulty imagining other possibilities. For that reason, instead of focusing on differential attraction of humans to other mammalian species, I will explore differential attraction *within* a species, using a species of non-human animals rather than humans. I particularly focus on attraction of baboons towards

FIGURE 5.2. Baboons, both individuals and groups, have been depicted very differently by different artists, as attractive by some, aversive by others. The subtle colours, choice of watercolour as the medium, and the poses depicted in the watercolour paintings of Deborah Ross, an artist who has spent much time observing and painting African wildlife, enhance the message of attraction. In contrast is the depiction of baboons by an unknown artist who used sharp lines and intense black and bold primary colours to show baboon males in threatening poses, reflecting the story theme of the film being promoted.

other baboons. What do we know about attraction in a species such as baboons? In what contexts do individuals demonstrate differential attraction? What characteristics, what traits, what senses do they use? Are their decisions similar to what yours or mine would be in the same circumstances?

A window on baboon life

For over forty years my colleagues and I have followed what is now seven generations of baboon families living in the Amboseli basin on the plains north and west of the base of Mount Kilimanjaro in southern Kenya.[1] The local Maasai pastoralists occasionally observe that baboons seem to be our cattle, but they are keen to point out that we have poor taste in our choice of cattle! We follow visually identified individuals – currently approximately 350 individuals living in 6 different groups; their close maternally related kin – mothers, sisters, daughters – and more recently, through genetic analysis, paternal relatives as well. Our research team, primarily from Kenya and the United States, aims to follow these individuals from birth to death. We collect many types of data, almost all of it 'hands-off' and non-invasively, following explicit protocols, for a range of investigations. Inevitably we also make more casual observations, which can prompt new formal investigations. Observers very quickly notice that some individuals have many sexual partners, playmates or friends, while others have few. Determining this is easier than answering the subsequent questions: on what basis do these individual differences occur and why? And what are the consequences?

Meet the baboons

Baboons are among the largest of monkeys and are our close relatives. Adult males weigh approximately twenty-five kilograms and adult females about half that. Baboons spend about the same proportion of time in each life stage as humans do, but each life stage and their total life span is about a third as long as those of humans. Even though most

---

[1] See https://amboselibaboons.nd.edu/ for an introduction to baboons and our research.

primates are considered social, baboons are among the most social species. Females live throughout their lives in the cohesive group into which they are born, what is often termed a matrilocal social group. Males, on the other hand, face the tough challenge of having to leave their home group. They are not forced by others to leave, but they choose to do so, and they spend their adulthood in one or more other groups. Such natal dispersal by one sex is the common pattern among many vertebrates. Baboons are also like many other mammals in having a mating system that is polygynandrous: both males and females have several mates. However, another characteristic of baboons is unusual, and is very much like humans: their reproduction is only minimally seasonal; that is, they reproduce at relatively high frequencies in all months of the year. That might not seem very important for our topic here. However, lack of seasonal reproduction means that infants are born, and potential mates join and leave groups, throughout the year. As a result, when youngsters begin to seek playmates, their potential partners tend to differ in age and background experience. These several characteristics taken together have important implications for considering differential attraction, including attraction to potential mates.

Mate attraction

Attraction to sexual partners, a topic of considerable public interest, is also a major topic of study in evolutionary biology because of its implications for differential reproductive success. For many species of birds, for example, we know that visual signals, particularly colour and pattern, serve as a major sexual advertisement and attractant. A few primates, such as the African mandrills and guenons, and some of the neo-tropical tamarin monkeys, are also colourful, and colours often differ both between species and among individuals within a species. Not surprisingly, for some primate species bright colours and associated displays are important in mate attraction. But most primates, including baboons and naked humans, are not colourful and are certainly no match for the flashy species. In widespread acknowledgement of this deficit, we humans have created a diversity of stylized adornments such as military uniforms and academic gowns, and we add colour to our dull bodies by using a broad range of clothing and make-up. The Maasai men and women who live on Amboseli's savannahs where we study baboons are remarkable in their ability to cover this relatively boring human body and hair with bright red ochre paint and cloth and ornamentation in primary colours, especially bright red and blue. But what is a non-human primate such as a baboon to do? How to look beautiful or attractive to other baboons? Not looking too showy can of course be an advantage when it comes to avoiding predation. Furthermore, having a bland appearance can reduce energetic costs because colourful traits tend to be expensive to produce and maintain. Still, this major source for signals of attraction appears greatly muted.

In our research, we distinguish hundreds of individual baboons by visual appearance, so baboons certainly differ in appearance even to humans. Possibly, we primates have a greater sensitivity to subtle visual differences than many other species do. Nonetheless, although both males and females have a pretty boring appearance much of the time, one striking visual characteristic of baboons and some other primates is that females have a very bold advertisement of their fertility: a shiny pink anogenital swelling (Figure 5.3) that changes with proximity to the time of ovulation (and somewhat with age). Males definitely pay attention to this signal. Male attraction is biased towards females with whom mating is likely to result in conception and successful offspring. Interestingly, in contrast to most human males, baboon males are not most attracted to the nubile adolescent females, despite the considerable effort of these adolescents to gain the males' attention, and despite the fact that the sexual swellings of the adolescents are what most human observers consider the more beautiful sex skins (for those of us who do think that some of these swellings are beautiful). Adolescent females repeatedly walk up to males and solicit sexual behaviour. The female virtually sticks her hindquarters in a male's face, but the adult male just ignores her, even turns away. One might say, 'But it would be so easy. Why don't the males accept the invitation?' I am unable to answer that question, but we can clearly say that adult male baboons are rarely interested. We know that the adolescent females are less fertile than adults who have produced young, and we also know that first offspring are less likely to survive than are later-born ones. The adult males behave as if they, too, know this. Rather than mating with adolescents, they prefer to spend their time foraging, thereby attaining better condition when potential sexual partners of higher reproductive quality become available. The preferred females, those who are fully adult and at peak fertility, exhibit swellings that many humans would consider unattractively grotesque. These are the sex-skin swellings that get the most attention from an adult male, and these swellings peak in size on cycles in which a female is more likely to conceive. So baboons and humans have a different sense of what is attractive, and the baboons' preferences better match fertility than do ours. In this instance, baboons may be 'smarter' than humans because the 'task' is a particularly relevant one to the baboon's real-life situation. In a species that is not monogamous and lives in groups where potential mates are sometimes a hundred metres away across the savannah, female visual signals and male sensitivity to them may be of considerable consequence and finely tuned.

FIGURE 5.3. Females of some primate species such as baboons exhibit highly visible 'sex-skin swellings' that are attractive to males.

Baboon males may also choose well because at close range they are receiving olfactory as well as visual information. Such chemical signals are a source of information not only about fertility but also about health, genetic relatedness and genetic diversity. This information can affect mate choice, providing a mechanism both for avoiding inbreeding and for promoting genetic diversity. Advances in methods for analysis of genetic and chemical material in faeces are enabling field researchers to 'get under the skin', without disturbing animals, and so to evaluate various aspects of genetics, physiology and other aspects of health. Genetic studies have demonstrated the animals' bias against mating with close paternally related as well as maternally related individuals. This is an example of attraction based not on a trait such as bright-pink sex skin, which identifies a partner that would be desirable to all, but a trait that leads to individual differences in attraction to an individual based on similarity (termed assortative mating), dissimilarity (disassortative mating) or other aspects of the relationship of one individual to another; a good partner for one individual is not necessarily a good one for another. Research that incorporates genetic as well as morphological and behavioural information about individuals is increasingly revealing other, more subtle, contributions of genetic characteristics to mate choice in nature.

Attraction to infants

From an evolutionary perspective, another important biological activity is ensuring that youngsters survive past infancy and into a safer life stage. It has long been observed that among primates, including humans, most individuals are intensely interested in infants. As soon as a baboon infant is born into its close-knit social group of about fifty animals it becomes the centre of attention, particularly but not exclusively by adult and juvenile females. One individual after another approaches and inspects the infant, then sits nearby uttering soft 'cohesion grunts'. If the infant's mother is not of very high social status, the other group members come right up and pull at the infant and particularly examine its genitals (Figure 5.4), which in baboons are very apparent. This ritual is similar to the response on entering a playground with a new-born human

A

B

FIGURE 5.4. Infants, both human and non-human, are highly attractive to other members of their group, especially so to adult and juvenile females. Adult males are disproportionately attracted to infants that genetic studies reveal the males have fathered. The mechanisms of this discrimination are not known, but the associations benefit the offspring in terms of support in peer fights and accelerated maturation.

infant – general attraction and great interest in knowing the infant's sex. "Is it a boy or a girl?" is the first thing that people want to know. I was sure when I first studied baboon infants that this genital inspection would lead to strong differential behaviour toward the two sexes, as occurs with humans, but neither I nor others have found evidence for such bias in natural non-human primate populations.

Rather than sex being the trait of primary interest during infant inspection, perhaps information gleaned about other traits is of more importance to the inspecting baboon as we saw it is in the case of mate choice – information about individual identity, genetic relatedness and health. Perhaps baboons, like humans, find some infants more attractive than others, based on traits such as large eyes, round face, symmetry of features, strength and clarity of vocalizations. Human infants are considered more attractive, and garner more care and positive responses, if their visual appearance, vocal signals and behaviour are more normal or healthy; this may be the case for non-human primates as well. In addition to visual and vocal signals, an inspecting baboon receives olfactory signals from an infant during close contact and inspection, particularly of the genital area, much as an adult male does when inspecting the hindquarters of potential sexual partners. The importance of olfaction in choice behaviour of humans and non-human primates has been increasingly recognized, due to a great extent to research that evaluates combinations of behaviour, olfaction, genetic diversity and genetic regions (MHC/HLA) that are particularly important in immune function and individual identity.

During the past decade research on several populations of wild and of semi-captive monkeys has documented strong discriminatory behaviour towards particular infants and juveniles. Strikingly, the helpful behaviour that baboon males direct towards neonates and their mothers is strongly biased in favour of their own genetic offspring and not just all infants of females with whom they mated half a year earlier. Among the baboons of Amboseli the fitness consequences of such bias is suggested by the earlier maturation of youngsters whose fathers stay in the group longer, rather than seeking new mating opportunities by emigrating to other baboon groups. Until these recent findings, conventional wisdom was that males in primate societies that have polygynandrous mating systems did not know which offspring were theirs, and did not provide paternal care. Now the question is: How do they know? To what extent do olfactory, visual, vocal, or other sources of information contribute to that knowledge? Also, seeing that male-to-infant attention is biased towards but not exclusively restricted to genetic relatives, another question is: Why isn't it better focused? Is the informational system imperfect, or do males have reasons other than paternal care for associating with youngsters? Several decades ago it was proposed that a male's caring behaviour towards an infant increases his future opportunities for mating with that infant's mother; however, data since then have not provided support for this interesting hypothesis.

Attraction to potential mating partners and to infants contributes to two cornerstones of evolutionary success, so the research focus on these two contexts is not surprising. But most primates, including most humans, spend relatively little of their lives as vulnerable infants or in trying to attract new mates. Are there other major contexts for differential intraspecific attractions? The study of friendship and social relationships in non-human primate juveniles and adults has a long and rich history in research on captive animals. Now, long-term studies of individually known members of natural populations are increasingly providing insights into the magnitude as well as the sources and consequences of such special relationships in nature.

Friendships: juvenile attraction to play partners

Like other mammalian young, juvenile primates are very playful, spontaneously and enthusiastically engaging in considerable amounts of locomotor and object play when energy resources allow. Like humans and many other highly social species, baboon youngsters also engage in much social play, and this play is widely thought to be an important component of preparation for social success during adulthood. Do baboon juveniles simply do a lot of playing and other social activities (Figure 5.5), with whoever is available, or do they bias their play towards particular partners much as human youngsters do? It has long been known that when young monkeys and young humans are given a choice of playmates, they prefer same-sex partners and those who are close to them in age, but

FIGURE 5.5. Juvenile non-human primates and humans are more attracted to playmates of the same age and sex than to others. However, they form play associations with others when ideal partners are not available, as often occurs in natural populations where group sizes are small and infants are born at all times of the year, rather than seasonally as in most mammals. Subtle differential attractions may sometimes still prevail in these situations. Behavioural adjustments may need to be made to maintain the play groups that do not 'ideally' reflect attractions. Little is known about the adult consequences of such variability during development.

these studies were primarily conducted with monkeys in captivity and with humans in modern contexts in which a diverse range of partners are usually available to choose from. However, in most traditional or rural human societies as well as in natural groups of wild-living non-human primates, youngsters often find themselves with few possible playmates, none that meet the 'ideal' criteria of same sex and age – recall that reproduction occurs at similar frequency throughout all months of the year resulting in births being scattered in time. Juveniles that, for example, were only willing to play with those who are very close in age might not find an acceptable playmate. Being too choosy about the age and sex (or genetic relatedness, about which less is known) could leave youngsters with no playmates. In fact, neither baboons nor human children forgo play when faced with a paucity of 'ideal' partners. Rather, they not only play with more diverse partners but they often adapt aspects of their play to these situations – for example by males or older partners engaging in less or more gentle rough-and-tumble play than they would otherwise do. For highly social species such as humans and many non-human primates, social play is probably essential for the success of group living. If so, youngsters' willingness to be flexible in their choice of playmates, and their ability to adapt their play to the challenges of play with less similar partners, may be as important to their success as are the advantages accrued by their attractions to and their preferences for similar partners when such partners are available to them. In addition, diversity of experience and of playmates early in life may in itself provide valuable payoffs during adulthood under some conditions. This may especially be the case in a variable or changing world.

The social life of young baboons gradually changes over the course of the several years that they spend as juveniles before becoming adolescents and then even full adults. This juvenile period sees increasing separation of the sexes as both males and females engage more in behaviours that characterize their very gender-differentiated lives as adults. Males experience the beginning of a growth spurt in body size and spend an increasing amount of their play time engaged in rough-and-tumble play, presaging the challenges of entering new groups and the high levels of ongoing male–male competition as adults. Females, in contrast, tend to spend more time than males in mutual grooming interactions and in interacting with new mothers and their infants. A major aspect of the increasing gender differences is evident in the attractions and partner roles during grooming interactions, interaction in which females are the major participants and that provide the 'social glue' of adult friendships.

Friendships: adult attractions to grooming partners

Throughout the life of baboons and most other primates, close proximity and affiliative contact such as huddling and social grooming are hallmarks of their activities when animals are not involved in the essential work of 'making a living' by foraging. Not surprisingly, the origins of close adult friendships may be found in the mother–infant relationship, starting during gestation. Primates' relatively long gestational period of intimate contact within the womb is followed in monkeys and apes by being carried throughout the day. For many primate infants, including baboons, this early post-natal period is an external extension of the pre-natal one because survival itself is contingent on constant contact as the infant clings to its mother's ventrum in a shady and protected position that provides easy access to the nipple and a full-time ride during the long day-journeys in search of food and water. From the first days, while resting, mothers also gently groom their infants' fur. And each night is spent with the infant being enveloped protectively in its mother's warm, soft cradle. Warm and caring contact, with its predominance of tactile as well as olfactory stimuli, may thereby provide one of the earliest and most enduring sources of attraction. Only later and gradually is such contact supplemented and partially replaced by longer distance visual and vocal cues as individuals spend less time in actual contact while they garner their own sustenance and provide their own transport.

During that first period of continuous intimate contact, the infant's social world, too, is provided by its mother – her friends become its friends and her enemies become the infant's enemies as well. Not surprising, then, that at least for a daughter the bond with her mother almost always remains one of her very closest as long as her mother is alive. Even after its first year of life when mother is not essential for a young baboon's survival and when the mother will soon be focused on her next infant, the two will often be found foraging and resting near each other during the day and perhaps huddling in the same cluster of animals in the sleeping trees at night. By the end of infancy, not only do mothers groom their infants, but daughters begin grooming their mothers, cementing their close social bond for the future by making the transition from a relationship characterized solely by parental care to the youngster's first reciprocal one. Over the next few years daughters' contribution to the relationship gradually grows to parity, whereas sons continue to solicit grooming from their mothers but only rarely provide grooming in return. What little grooming young males do is increasingly directed towards others rather than their mothers. Thus, even before sex differences in play are evident, gender differences emerge in grooming behaviour and the partners to which the youngsters are attracted.

What is so special about grooming? What is this 'social glue'? Grooming requires the groomer's full attention as she or he 'combs' through the partner's fur, examining skin and hair for ectoparasites and detritus that are then removed. Being groomed well is somewhat like receiving a massage or having one's hair carefully plaited (Figure 5.6). The intimate hands-on contact of grooming requires both a high degree of trust on the part of the one being groomed and focused effort on the part of a good groomer. Such physical closeness, the recipient relaxed and often with eyes closed, makes for a potentially vulnerable situation. Strikingly, early experimental studies of captive primates found that stronger grooming relationships were associated with physiological

FIGURE 5.6. Adult female baboons exhibit differentiated social relationships; they have strong social relationships with some particular adult females and not with others. Here, human friends and family members engage in the relaxed and relaxing hands-on grooming behaviour that is also the most time-consuming affiliative social behaviour in baboons, also shown grooming. Females of both species are strongly attracted to forming close bonds with some individuals and not with others. Image on left courtesy of Stuart Altmann.

profiles characteristic of lower stress. Individuals concentrate these close physical relationships on a select few of their acquaintances. Among baboon females, these close bonds or friendships are formed to a considerable extent with close genetic relatives (mothers, daughters and sisters) rather than partners being chosen based on traits such as particular size or voice that would lead to all individuals seeking close bonds with the same few others. However, if a female has few close relatives, or none, she will form close bonds with non-relatives rather than forgo friendships, much as juveniles seek playmates even when no favoured playmates are available; friendships seem to be that important. The basis of whether and with whom individuals form friendships with non-relatives is not yet well understood, but some insights come from the finding that social bonds among adult females that are more reciprocal are also stronger and more enduring, suggesting characteristics that might make some partners attractive. Ontogenetically, these friendships may have their origins in the play and grooming relationships during the juvenile years. Recent research is also beginning to reveal valuable long-term consequences, fitness advantages, of these friendships among adult females. In Amboseli, offspring of baboon mothers who have a greater number of friendships have better survival chances. And in the Moremi baboon population in Botswana, adult females themselves experience higher rates of survival if they have more friends. These benefits are evident even after controlling for other potentially important effects such as a female's social status (dominance rank in baboons) and the number of close relatives she has. This finding provides another example of differential attractions having important evolutionary consequences. In this case physiological benefits may provide one proximate mechanism by which strong social bonds contribute to longevity.

A 'feeling for the organism' and awareness of ourselves

At each life stage and in diverse areas of activity, individuals exhibit strong attractions – often strong differential attractions to some and not others in their social world. Several themes emerge from our sampling of attractions in the life of baboons and are common to other species.

One major theme relates to the basis of attraction, whether it is based on 'absolute best' or an 'ideal match'. Sometimes all individuals prefer the same absolute traits – for example all being attracted to the largest sexual swellings or perhaps the healthiest-appearing youngsters or the individual who gives the most thorough grooming. At other times preference is for those who bear some relationship to the evaluator – perhaps genetic similarity or difference or an optimal position along that continuum; or perhaps similarity in size rather than the largest; or perhaps a mate and child-rearing partner with dissimilar, complementary traits rather than traits that duplicate those of the chooser. The evolutionary consequences of these two different bases are of particular importance.

A second theme bears on the sensory modalities that individuals use in determining attraction and beauty, the contributions of different modalities and the range of differences that are important to choosers. Visual and vocal sources of beauty receive widespread attention from human adults in their personal lives, particularly in attraction to mates and in reaction to infants. And scientists as human adults often naturally start with attention to these modalities, which are well developed and acknowledged in humans and other primates. Does it matter if we focus on just some senses or just some ranges of some senses, the ones that match our own skills? Do we come away with very different pictures of attraction, of beauty, than a member of another species might?

A striking example comes from olfactory cues. Most scientists come from relatively modern industrial countries where olfaction is not a 'nice' topic. Unless you are growing roses in your garden or choosing perfumes, we do not generally comment about a person smelling good. We are more likely to comment on a person smelling bad, usually associated with deficiencies in bathing. We tend not to explore that part of our sensory world. We may not be as sensitive to olfactory cues as dogs or even baboons are, but we still have a considerable olfactory capability, and olfaction is starting to receive more research attention for primates, including humans. We can each probably think of olfactory examples from our childhood, particular odours – such as baking bread, pots of soup, the smell of approaching rain that ends a drought – that stand out and draw us towards situations and people that exhibit those characteristics. For me, this is the smell of roasting coffee – my grandfather had a little coffee importing and roasting shop in Greenwich Village in New York, and I spent many happy hours there and in my grandparents' flat above the shop. Mail from my grandparents always smelled of roasting coffee; decades later, it remains a beautiful odour to me. My children have a similar reaction to the odours associated with Maasai handiwork. Attractive odours vary by individuals, by cultures, and surely across history. The importance of the tactile modality, of contact – caring, protective stress-reducing, temperature-regulating contact versus the lack of contact or infliction of harsh, even violent contact – remains largely unstudied outside the realm of rearing conditions characterized by extreme deprivation especially in humans and other primates. Those extremes and contrasting examples such as that of baboon grooming suggest a fertile area for both improving scientific understanding and application to enhancing well-being of humans and other animals.

How much are scientists' ideas of attractive characteristics also affected by the changing capabilities of the measurement tools we use and the context in which we can use those tools? One of the areas in which this has been particularly striking is in the study of vocal cues and other sounds. Many sounds that are important to other species, whether small rodents or enormous elephants, are outside our range of hearing, for example extremely high sounds in the case of small rodents, and very low ones in the case of elephants. For a long time, people were not even aware of much of the auditory world of these species. For some species there are wonderful stories of the first discoveries of this other world of attractions when combinations of sensitive observers, ones with a 'feeling for the organism' and emerging technologies led scientists to it. Technological advances too have made it possible to record and experiment with sounds in animals' natural habitats, opening up a rich mine of knowledge that will continue to reveal greater understanding of vocal attractions and repulsions much more complex and individual than traditionally explored.

Finally, developing attractions and sense of beauty are a lifetime affair. For some species certain attractions are determined during a brief, so-called critical period – for example the bond between a young duckling, fawn, goat, or wildebeest and its caretaker that occurs through 'imprinting' shortly after birth. For humans and other primates such as baboons and many other mammals, however, attractions are first formed in utero and continue to be shaped throughout our lives. They reflect our experiences with our physical and social world. Their origins go even further back in time than our foetal life as we absorb and integrate and shape into our own version the attractions and repulsions of our mothers, our other caregivers, and the entirety of our social world. At every stage these experiences interact with our genetic make-up as well, helping shape the expression of genes and contributing to what our attractions will become. And so it is with other species and in other times and places. All our senses – including tactile, auditory, visual, olfactory – contribute. From conception to birth and beyond, these senses develop on different schedules and with different sensitivities and ranges, establishing initial but changing biases. They contribute differentially at different moments in life, differently for different species and populations and even among individuals.

The examples of attraction among baboons strongly remind us that what is attractive to one individual may not be to another, because of the strong evolutionary importance of genetic relatedness for many aspects of behaviour, the potentially great variability in individual sensitivity to various stimuli, and different experiences during ontogeny. Indeed, beauty is in all of the senses and the mind of the beholder. How much we share with each other, with other species, and how much they with each other we will come to know only as we continue to expand our search for beauty and attraction in the many corners where they reside. Doing so will benefit from an interplay among scientific method, technological advances, intuition and a 'feeling for the organism'. As we expand our understanding of beauty, we will learn both more about ourselves and more about other species.

6 Beauty and happiness: Chinese perspectives

JASON C. KUO

When I received the invitation to speak as part of the Darwin College lecture series on *Beauty*, I was deeply conscious of the honour paid me, but apprehensive. I was afraid I had nothing new or original to say, because both beauty and happiness have been discussed or represented by philosophers and artists at different times and places throughout human history. As I prepared my lecture, I also remembered what Walter Pater wrote in 1893 in his preface to *The Renaissance: Studies in Art and Poetry*: 'Beauty, like all other qualities presented to human experience, is relative; and the definition of it becomes unmeaning and useless in proportion to its abstractness.'[1]

As a postgraduate fellow at the Freer Gallery of Art in Washington in the late 1970s, every day I had to use an entrance hidden behind one of the walls of the Peacock Room (Figure 6.1) to reach my small office. The Peacock Room was designed by James Whistler (1834–1903) as the dining room for his patron, Frederick Richards Leyland (1831–92); it was later dismantled and was sold eventually to Charles Lang Freer (1854–1919). In 1923 it was reinstalled in the Freer Gallery of Art. Seeing the Peacock Room daily gave me ample opportunity to think about beauty and happiness. First of all, it compelled me to contemplate what the French writer Stendhal wrote on several occasions: beauty is nothing other than the promise of happiness.[2] It also reminded me of John Ruskin's assertion in *Stones of Venice*: 'Remember that the most

---

[1] Walter Pater, *The Renaissance: Studies in Art and Poetry*, ed. Donald L. Hill (Berkeley and Los Angeles: University of California Press, 1980), xix.

[2] 'La beauté n'est jamais, ce me semble, qu'une *promesse de bonheur*': Stendhal, *Rome, Naples et Florence* (Paris: Champion, 1919), vol. I, 45–46; 'La beauté n'est que la *promesse* du bonheur': *De l'amour* (Paris: Champion, 1967), vol. I, 74, n1.

FIGURE 6.1. Peacock Room, Freer Gallery, Washington, DC

beautiful things in the world are the most useless; peacock and lilies, for instance.'[3] The blue and white porcelains in the Peacock Room also evoked the 'china-mania' initiated by Whistler and his contemporaries. The fact that blue-and-white porcelain, most of it mass produced in Chinese factories for export and considered quite unremarkable by Chinese connoisseurs, caused such a sensation in Europe from the seventeenth century onward made me wonder if there is such a thing as universal beauty.

A study of young women's faces, published in the *British Journal of Psychology* in 1960, and a similar study conducted in the United States (published in *Sociology and Social Research* in 1965) seemed to indicate that 'people in the same culture agree strongly about who is beautiful and who

[3] *Stones of Venice*, 1851–3, vol. I, 2.17; quoted in Linda Merrill, *The Peacock Room* (New Haven: Yale University Press, 1998), epigraph.

is not'.[4] Do these studies lead one to conclude that there is a universal conception of physical beauty? Charles Darwin, very much aware of the diversity of beauty, provided an answer: 'If everyone were cast in the same mould, there would be no such thing as beauty.'[5] In the moulds from which the mass-produced porcelains were cast we have a striking illustration of Darwin's assertion.

If we look to the origins of this manufactured aesthetic, we can see in Chinese art an embodiment of some of the most important legacies of Chinese civilization for the modern world: the importance of education and the educability of all people; a profound respect for nature; and an emphasis on human – individual and collective – good. Moreover, China has one of the longest continuous artistic traditions in the world, and that tradition has contributed to visual culture an endless stream of great masters, glorious monuments, and intriguing theories about art and beauty. Chinese civilization has also produced fascinating ideas about the pursuit of happiness.

I would like to begin with those associated with the Daoist philosopher Zhuangzi, who lived in the fourth century BCE. The ideas of Zhuangzi and his followers were collected in the Daoist classic *Zhuangzi*, and they have given rise to a long tradition of scepticism, anti-traditionalism, iconoclasm and unorthodoxy in regard to the pursuit of beauty and happiness. Whenever I gaze at the goldfish swimming below the Flying Rainbow Bridge in the sixteenth-century Garden of the Unsuccessful Politician in Suzhou (Figure 6.2), I am reminded of a parable from *Zhuangzi*:

> Zhuangzi and Huizi were strolling along the dam of the Hao River when Zhuangzi said, 'See how the minnows come out and dart around where they please! That's what fish really enjoy!'
> Huizi said, 'You're not a fish – how do you know what fish enjoy?'
> Zhuangzi said, 'You're not I, so how do you know I don't know what fish enjoy?'
> Huizi said, 'I'm not you, so I certainly don't know what you know. On the other hand, you're certainly not a fish – so that still proves you don't know what fish enjoy!'

[4] Nancy Eticoff, *Survival of the Prettiest: The Science of Beauty* (New York: Anchor Books, 2000), 137.

[5] Charles Darwin, *The Descent of Man and Selection in Relation to Sex* (Princeton: Princeton University Press, 1981), ii, 354.

FIGURE 6.2. Flying Rainbow Bridge, Garden of the Unsuccessful Politician, Suzhou.

> Zhuangzi said, 'Let's go back to your original question, please. You asked me how I know what fish enjoy – so you already knew I knew it when you asked the question. I know it by standing here beside the Hao.'[6]

One of the most well-known passages from *Zhuangzi* is that about the Butterfly's Dream:

> Zhuang Zhou [Zhuangzi] dreamt he was a butterfly, a butterfly flitting and fluttering around, happy with himself and doing as he pleased. He didn't know he was Zhuang Zhou. Suddenly he woke up and there he was, solid and unmistakable Zhuang Zhou. But he didn't know if he was Zhuang Zhou who had dreamt he was a butterfly, or a butterfly dreaming he was Zhuang Zhou. Between Zhuang Zhou and a butterfly there must be some distinction! This is called the Transformation of Things.[7]

Both the parable about the enjoyment of fish and the passage about the Butterfly's Dream exemplify the Daoist belief in the subjectivity of

---

[6] Trans. in Burton Watson, *The Complete Works of Chuang Tzu*, romanization modified; accessed at www.terebess.hu/english/chuangtzu.html.
[7] Ibid.

happiness and beauty. A passage from the chapter 'Discussion on making all things equal' in *Zhuangzi* further indicates the Daoist scepticism about the objectivity of beauty:

> Men claim that Mao Qiang and Lady Li were beautiful, but if fish saw them they would dive to the bottom of the stream, if birds saw them they would fly away, and if deer saw them they would break into a run. Of these four, which knows how to fix the standard of beauty for the world?[8]

Zhuangzi's scepticism about the objectivity of beauty can be seen in the popularity of a series of paintings of 'beautiful women'. These were displayed at the exhibition China: The Three Chinese Emperors, 1662–1795 at the Royal Academy of Arts in London in 2006 and have been among the most popular pieces in exhibitions organized for Western audiences, perhaps because they seem to exemplify the idealized life of women and the ideal of feminine beauty in China. Painted by anonymous court artists for Prince Yinzhen, the future Yongzheng emperor who would rule China from 1722 to 1735, these pictures reveal the persistence of many Westerners' curiosity about what lies behind the doors of the Forbidden City. Many of the pictures contain sexual innuendo; in one example, 'one woman is courted by a pair of magpies who call to her through the window; together the magpies represent a conventional sign for "double happiness," a symbol of the conjugal bliss of a wedded couple; but the woman sits alone waiting'.[9] The screen, truncated by the frame, also features one hundred forms of the same Chinese character *shou*, or 'long life'. Double happiness and long life are what every man and woman would like to have.

The popularity of these kinds of pictures with Western audiences is not new. Starting with the Greek myth of the luxury and decadence of Asia, through Marco Polo's account of the gorgeous 'East', to the French writer Victor Segalen's literary encounter with and 're-creation' of Chinese art, the story of Westerners' changing images, perceptions, impressions and constructions of Chinese art is a history of mutual misunderstanding and understanding between 'East' and 'West'. One of

---

[8] Ibid.

[9] Jan Stuart *et al.*, *China: The Three Chinese Emperors, 1662–1795* (London: Royal Academy of Arts, 2006), 431–2.

FIGURE 6.3. Ceramic bowl, David Foundation, London.

the most telling examples is Hegel's assertion on Chinese painting in his lectures in the 1820s on the philosophy of history:

> The Chinese have not yet succeeded in representing the beautiful as beautiful; for in their painting shadow and perspective are wanting ... the Exalted, the Ideal and the Beautiful are not the domain of [the Chinese artist's] art and skill.[10]

In the writings on Chinese art by some of the most perceptive modern art historians and critics – Roger Fry, Clement Greenberg, Ernest Gombrich, and Arthur Danto – the trope of 'difference' is unmistakable. Roger Fry, in particular, is an excellent example of Western critics' understanding as well as their difficulty in comprehending some unique aspects of the Chinese sense of beauty. Fry's shrewd insight can be seen in his appreciation, first published in 1919, of a ceramic bowl from the Song dynasty that is now in the collection of the David Foundation in London (Figure 6.3):

> We apprehend gradually the shape of the outside contour, the perfect sequence of the curves, and the subtle modification of a certain type of curve which it shows; we also feel the relation of the concave curves of the

---

[10] Georg Wilhelm Friedrich Hegel, *The Philosophy of History*, trans. J. Sibree (Buffalo, NY: Prometheus Books, 1991 (repr.)), 116; also quoted in part by Arthur Danto, 'The Work of Art and the Historical Future', in *'Anything Goes': The Work of Art and the Historical Future* (Berkeley: Townsend Center for the Humanities, University of California 1998), 3.

inside to the outside contour; we realize that the precise thickness of the walls is consistent with the particular kind of matter of which it is made, its appearance of density and resistance; and finally we recognize, perhaps, how satisfactory for the display of all these plastic qualities are the color and dull lustre of the glaze.[11]

In one of his last lectures as the Slade Professor of Fine Arts at Cambridge University (1933–4), Fry compared Chinese art with the art of other ancient civilizations:

> But in early Chinese art we shall find the balance between geometric regularity and sensibility is of an almost unique kind. I think we may say that in no period in Chinese art has sensibility been completely repressed. The notion of the organization of form and of its perfection has never with them implied – as it so often has elsewhere – the suppression of sensibility.[12]

As we shall see in a minute, Chinese calligraphy occupies a unique and supreme position in Chinese art. Fry intuitively sensed its importance when he repeatedly talked about 'linear rhythm' in Chinese art. He wrote:

> [A] Chinese picture ... never loses the evidence of the linear rhythm as the main method of expression. And this is only natural, the medium used being always some kind of water-colour and the art of painting being always regarded as a part of the art of *calligraphy*. A painting was always conceived as the visible record of a rhythm gesture. It was the graph of a dance executed by the hand.[13]

However, Fry did not go any further in exploring the significance of calligraphy in the Chinese sense of beauty.

In 1956, when the Chinese artist Zhang Ding visited Paris, he met Picasso, who remarked that, had he been born Chinese, he would have been a calligrapher.[14] The pre-eminence of calligraphy in the Chinese sense of beauty raises important questions about the categorization of the

---

[11] First published in *The Athenaeum* in 1919, reprinted in Roger Fry, *Vision and Design* (Cleveland: World Publishing, 1956 [1920]), 49–50.

[12] Roger Fry, *Last Lectures*, intro. by Kenneth Clark, first published by Cambridge University Press in 1939 (Boston: Beacon Press, 1962), 100.

[13] Roger Fry, 'The Significance of Chinese Art', in Roger Fry *et al., Chinese Art* (London: B. T. Batsford, 1935), 1–5 (emphasis added).

[14] Gordon S. Barrass, *The Art of Calligraphy in Modern China* (Berkeley and Los Angeles: University of California Press, 2002), 54.

arts and the problem of defining beauty in general. In China, calligraphy has traditionally been regarded as the most important and demanding in the hierarchy of the visual arts. As the Princeton Sinologist Frederick W. Mote put it in his preface to *Calligraphy and the East Asian Book*, Chinese calligraphy as an art form owes its special character to the nature of the Chinese script itself:

> Its forms are capable of a vast range of extension and variation; subject to the discipline of tradition and the inventiveness of personal style, for which alphabetic scripts in the Western tradition offer no counterpart.[15]

However, 'calligraphy' (Gk. *kalligraphia*, from *kalos* beautiful + *graphein* to write) is something of a misnomer in reference to Chinese art, in part because Chinese writing does not involve a simple alphabet of a few dozen symbols; it embraces some 50,000 distinct graphs, giving it a level of diversity and complexity not to be compared with any other modern languages. Sinologists have used the familiar term 'calligraphy' simply to create a convenient English-language equivalent.

Of all kinds of Chinese artefacts collected by Westerners, calligraphy has been the least understood and, until the past few decades, there have been very few collections of Chinese calligraphy.[16] Yet it has exerted one of the strongest influences on twentieth-century Euro-American art. In 1938 Chiang Yee published his book *Chinese Calligraphy: An Introduction to its Aesthetic and Technique*, based on his lectures at the School of Oriental and African Studies, University of London, during the great International Exhibition of Chinese art in London in 1935–6.[17] His book was very successful; it attracted the attention of Sir Herbert Read, who wrote the preface to the second edition in 1954 and noted the influence of Chinese calligraphy on artists in a 'new movement of painting' in post-war Europe, which included artists such as Pierre Soulages, Georges Mathieu and Hans Hartung. Chinese calligraphy has also been the source of

---

[15] Mote's preface to Frederick W. Mote and Hung-lam Chu, *Calligraphy and the East Asian Book* (Boston: Shambhala, 1989), 5.

[16] Qianshen Bai, Craig Shaw and Uta Lauer, 'Chinese Calligraphy Meets the West', in Ouyang Zhongshi, Wen Fong *et al.*, *Chinese Calligraphy*, ed. and trans. Wang Youfen (New Haven: Yale University Press, 2008), 439–61.

[17] Chiang Yee, *Chinese Calligraphy: An Introduction to its Aesthetic and Technique* (London: Methuen & Company, 1938).

influence, inspiration and exploration for many modern and contemporary American artists – Jackson Pollock, Mark Tobey and Brice Marden, to name just a few. One may speculate that Chinese calligraphy (together with its 'ideograms') served as a means to an end for the Euro-American artists in their search for their own alternative aesthetics.

There are superficial similarities between the eighth-century Buddhist monk Huaisu's (737–85) cursive hand scroll, *Autobiography* (dated 777), and Jackson Pollock's paintings from the 1950s. Huaisu's work is described as being done in a 'rapid, uninterrupted flow of darting, looping brush movement'.[18] In addition to the formal quality of speed, improvisation and spontaneity, Huaisu's calligraphy is itself a discursive literary text. For example, in *Autobiography* Huaisu quotes poetic couplets by Lu Xiang, Wang Yong and Zhu Yao respectively, three of his own contemporary critics who comment on his art:

> At first [the characters] appear as mist, gently descending over old pines;
>
> Then they transform into peaks that cleave the sky. (Lines 68–70, Figure 6.4A)
>
> [The characters are like] monkeys in winter, shaking up withered vines while drinking water;
>
> [The characters are like] strong men plucking up hills, or flexing iron with all their might. (Lines 71–3, Figure 6.4B)
>
> When [Huaisu] set the brush down, one could only make out flashes of lightning;
>
> The characters completed, one was merely afraid, coiling dragons might rise up. (Lines 74–7, Figure 6.4C)[19]

While Pollock's paintings are primarily appreciated for their non-representational surface, anyone who has some knowledge of the Chinese cursive script can retrace in the mind or even repeat on paper the process by which Huaisu's work was originally done. Huaisu created his work in the cosmopolitan society of the Tang empire and its flamboyant and

---

[18] Wen C. Fong *et al.*, *Possessing the Past: Treasures from the National Palace Museum* (New York: Metropolitan Museum of Art, 1996), 118.

[19] Adapted from Adele Schlombs, *Huai-su and the Beginnings of Wild Cursive Script in Chinese Calligraphy* (Stuttgart: Franz Steiner, 1998), 53–4.

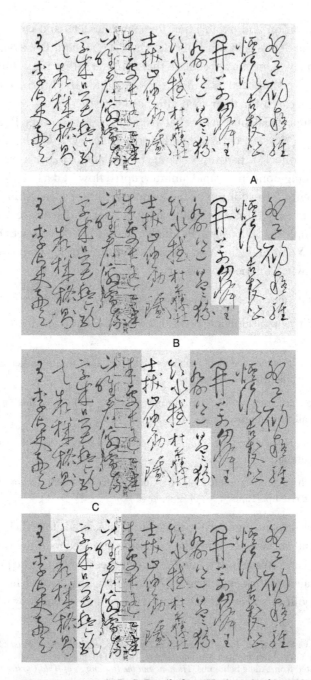

FIGURE 6.4. A, B, C, Details from Huaisu, *Autobiography*, Taipei. From Gugong Shuhua Tulu (Taipei: National Palace Museum, 1991).

self-confident culture in the eighth century. Through his extremely dynamic and highly eccentric version of cursive script, the *kuangcao* (wild or crazy cursive script), Huaisu went down in Chinese history as a paragon of beauty, artistic freedom and excellence. Although Huaisu was a Buddhist monk, his art of the 'wild or crazy cursive script' was mainly inspired by the Daoist approach to art and beauty. Zhuangzi, the Daoist philosopher discussed above, rarely talks about the fine arts as such, but there are several parables that became central to an understanding of later Chinese thinking about beauty and the pursuit of happiness. First is the parable about Cook Ding, from chapter 3 of *Zhuangzi*:

> Cook Ding was cutting up an ox for Lord Wen-hui. At every touch of his hand, every heave of his shoulder, every move of his feet, every thrust of his knee – zip! zoop! He slithered the knife along with a zing, and all was in perfect rhythm, as though he were performing the dance of the Mulberry Grove or keeping time to the Jingshou music.
>
> 'Ah, this is marvelous!' said Lord Wenhui. 'Imagine skill reaching such heights!'
>
> Cook Ding laid down his knife and replied, 'What I care about is the Way, which goes beyond skill. When I first began cutting up oxen, all I could see was the ox itself. After three years I no longer saw the whole ox. And now – now I go at it by spirit and don't look with my eyes. Perception and understanding have come to a stop and spirit moves where it wants. I go along with the natural makeup, strike in the big hollows, guide the knife through the big openings, and follow things as they are. So I never touch the smallest ligament or tendon, much less a main joint.
>
> 'A good cook changes his knife once a year – because he cuts. A mediocre cook changes his knife once a month – because he hacks. I've had this knife of mine for nineteen years and I've cut up thousands of oxen with it, and yet the blade is as good as though it had just come from the grindstone. There are spaces between the joints, and the blade of the knife has really no thickness. If you insert what has no thickness into such spaces, then there's plenty of room – more than enough for the blade to play about it. That's why after nineteen years the blade of my knife is still as good as when it first came from the grindstone.
>
> 'However, whenever I come to a complicated place, I size up the difficulties, tell myself to watch out and be careful, keep my eyes on what I'm doing, work very slowly, and move the knife with the greatest subtlety, until – flop! the whole thing comes apart like a clod of earth crumbling to the ground. I stand there holding the knife and look all

around me, completely satisfied and reluctant to move on, and then I wipe off the knife and put it away.'

'Excellent!' said Lord Wen-hui. 'I have heard the words of Cook Ding and learned how to care for life!'[20]

The second parable is about the woodworker Qing, from chapter 19 of *Zhuangzi*:

> Woodworker Qing carved a piece of wood and made a bell stand, and when it was finished, everyone who saw it marveled, for it seemed to be the work of gods or spirits. When the marquis of Lu saw it, he asked, 'What art is it you have?'
>
> Qing replied, 'I am only a craftsman – how would I have any art? There is one thing, however. When I am going to make a bell stand, I never let it wear out my energy. I always fast in order to still my mind. When I have fasted for three days, I no longer have any thought of congratulations or rewards, of titles or stipends. When I have fasted for five days, I no longer have any thought of praise or blame, of skill or clumsiness. And when I have fasted for seven days, I am so still that I forget I have four limbs and a form and body. By that time, the ruler and his court no longer exist for me. My skill is concentrated and all outside distractions fade away. After that, I go into the mountain forest and examine the Heavenly nature of the trees. If I find one of superlative form, and I can see a bell stand there, I put my hand to the job of carving; if not, I let it go. This way I am simply matching up "Heaven" with "Heaven." That's probably the reason that people wonder if the results were not made by spirits.'[21]

Perhaps one of the most fascinating artists who exemplifies the Daoist approach to art is the eighth-century painter Wu Daozi. The ninth-century critic Zhang Yanyuan summarized the style of Wu Daozi's figure painting in this manner:

> And therefore such was the virile manifestation of spirit-resonance that it could scarcely be contained upon painting silk; such was the rugged freedom of his brushwork that he had to give free expression to his ideas on the wall.[22] ... Wu Daozi was endowed by Heaven with a vigorous brushwork, and even as a youth he had acquired the divine mysteries of the art, ... employing according to his fancy strange rocks that

---

[20] Trans. in Watson, *The Complete Works of Chuang Tzu*.
[21] Ibid.
[22] Trans. in William Acker, *Some T'ang and Pre-T'ang Texts on Chinese Painting* (Leiden: Brill, 1954), vol. I, 151–2.

looked as though one might touch them, and rushing torrents from which it seemed one might dip water.[23]

To understand better Wu Daozi's stylistic origins, however, one has to turn to his training in calligraphy, for the greatest achievement of Wu Daozi, according to Zhang Yanyuan, lay in his brushwork.[24] And as the ninth-century critic Zhu Jingxuan pointed out, 'what is incomparable is his brushwork, which is always profusely varied and full of an untrammelled energy'.[25] Like Huaisu, Wu Daozi learned calligraphy from Zhang Xu.[26] Zhang Xu, called Shudian or 'Calligraphy Eccentric' and Caosheng or 'Sage of Cursive Calligraphy' by his contemporaries, achieved a personal style that was uniquely energetic, full of movement and charged with force, even within a single stroke.[27] As Wu Daozi studied with him, one can expect that Zhang Xu's style of calligraphy, marked by an extravagant rendering of brushwork and rapid execution, might have exerted a decisive influence on Wu Daozi's style of figure painting.[28]

A number of stone engravings have been suggested as probably being based on the design or style of Wu Daozi.[29] The engraving (Figure 6.5) on the terrace of the Douwangdien ('Basilica of the King of Dou') at Quyang, Hebei, is particularly interesting.[30] It depicts a mountain spirit who, as the inscription on the stone tells us, is 'flying down like a white devil with a spear. Swift as wind he descends from the clouds to kill and to strike; an agent of Heaven, who deals out punishment and clears up secrets, so that the country and the people may be peaceful for ever'.[31] The figure, with its thinning and thickening of ever-moving line-work, gains an intense life of its own, swelling and bursting through the powerful and plastic realization of the demoniacal form.

---

[23] Ibid., 56.
[24] Ibid., 177–84.
[25] Trans. in Alexander C. Soper, 'T'ang Ch'ao Ming Hua Lu', *Artibus Asiae*, 21/3–4 (1958), 21.
[26] Acker, *Texts*, vol. II, 232.
[27] Toyama Gunji, 'Cho Kyoku ni tsuite', in *Shodo zenshu*, 25 vols. (Tokyo: Heibonsha, 1954–7), vol. VIII, 28–32.
[28] Acker, *Texts*, vol. II, 232.
[29] Osvald Sirén, *Chinese Painting: Leading Masters and Principles* (London: Lund Humphries, 1958), vol. I, 109–25.
[30] Ibid., vol. III, pl. 88.
[31] Sirén, *Chinese Painting*, vol. I, 114.

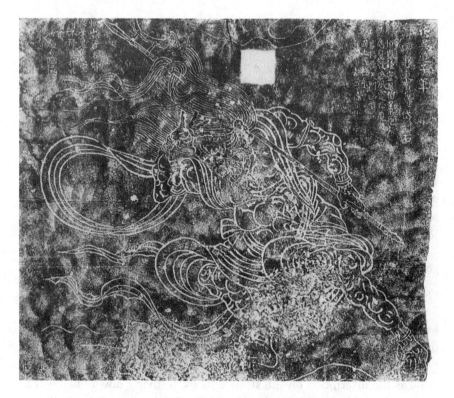

FIGURE 6.5. Wu Daozi, *Mountain Spirit*, Hebei.

Two stories about Wu Daozi are instructive about Chinese approaches to art. In the first story, he once painted a landscape on the wall of the palace but did not reveal it to the emperor until it was finished. He then pointed to a grotto in the painting and clapped his hands. A door opened, and the artist stepped into the picture and vanished with it in front of the emperor. In the second story, he painted five dragons on the walls of the palace; every time that rain fell, vapour rose from these pictures.[32] Unlike his predecessors who were more interested in realism, Wu Daozi brought about a more dynamic and spontaneous expression through swirling monochrome and ink-washes. This change paved the way for the rise of the *yipin* or 'untrammelled style' in painting in the late Tang dynasty

[32] Roger Goepper, *The Essence of Chinese Painting*, trans. Michael Bullock (London: Lund Humphries, 1963), 24, 26.

(618–907).[33] Since that time, the 'untrammelled style' has appeared throughout Chinese art history, from the literati artists of the Song dynasty (960–1279) to contemporary artists in the Chinese diaspora, such as Gao Xingjian in Paris. As the Japanese art historian Shimada Shujiro puts it:

> The *yipin* style began by emancipating painting from the orthodox mode which 'conformed to the object in portraying form' through the use of firm, fine brushwork; it stood in direct opposition to that mode. Whenever there arose a dissatisfaction with orthodoxy in painting, whenever something new was sought outside its pale, in whatever period, something of an *yipin* nature was apt to be born.[34]

Through the uses of inks of different intensities and shades and ever-changing brushwork, Guo Xi's *Early Spring*, signed and dated 1072 (Figure 6.6), has created an effect of dreamlike illusion of lights and shadows, suggesting a landscape where the trees are in dense mist when the winter is over and the spring is coming.

The contours of the mountains and rocks are not sharply delineated; rather, the tops of the mountains are revealed by the trees behind the clouds. Guo Xi's mastery of ink and brush is shown not only in his treatment of misty clouds, the chiaroscuro of the mountains, and the shapes of the tree trunks and old roots, but also in the strategic placement of people in the landscape. The British artist Julian Bell has written sensitively about this painting:

> You must wander your way through his brushwork slowly – budge right round the challenging foreground rocks to the bridge where a diminutive figure sets the scale; clamber up past the waterfall, where the homely roofs of a town await you; but now you have lost all access to the equally enticing deep valley on the left, while the dizzy peaks float out of your reach like so many dreams in the morning. All that binds the image together is the painter's responsiveness to the head-to-foot length of silk confronting him, as if its blankness were alive, as if each brushstroke must wrest from that fabric the life infusing the object at hand ... For an equivalent speculative tone and sense of personal experiment, European art would have to wait four centuries till the time of Leonardo.[35]

---

[33] Shimada Shujiro, 'Ippin gafu ni tsuite', *Bijutsu kenkyu*, 161 (1950), 20–46; trans. James Cahill, 'Concerning the I-p'in Style of Painting', *Oriental Art*, NS, 7 (1961), 66–74; 8 (1962), 130–7; and 10 (1964), 19–26.

[34] Trans. in Cahill, 'Concerning the I-p'in Style of Painting' (1964), 10.

[35] Julian Bell, *Mirror of the World: A New History of Art* (London: Thames & Hudson, 2007), 128–9.

FIGURE 6.6. Guo Xi, *Early Spring*, Taipei. From Gugong Shuhua Tulu
(Taipei: National Palace Museum, 1991).

Building on his experience and understanding of Wu Daozi and Guo Xi on whose work he wrote insightful comments, the late eleventh-century statesman and artist Su Shi (1037–1101), also known as Su Dongpo, developed a theory of literati painting (*wenrenhua*) which was greatly shaped by his experience in Daoism as well as Chan, one of the sects of Buddhism, which in turn had incorporated a great many Daoist ideas about the creative process. Just as Chan generally downplayed the importance of the preparatory discipline, so too Su Dongpo downplayed any specifically artistic training that might be necessary for the scholar-painter. He wrote:

> Why should a high-minded man study painting?
> The use of the brush comes naturally to him.
> It is like the case of those who are good at swimming;
> Each one of them could handle a boat.[36]

But just as the Chan master built on a strongly established sense of discipline in leading the student towards enlightenment, so too did Su turn to the scholar's training in calligraphy as an artistic foundation, for every educated Chinese would have mastered the discipline of the writing-brush. Here the mastery comes when there is no longer any conscious control or direction of the brush, when the cause of the mind and the effect of the brush's movement are absorbed into a spontaneous unity that must be experienced in order to be understood. As the discipline of Chan living freed the mind for enlightenment, so did mastery of the brush free the hand to catch faithfully the vision that was found in the mind. It was free to 'do', because its discipline had mastered the problem of 'how'. Chan enlightenment and artistic revelation were thus both based on the foundation of an underlying discipline that had to be first mastered. Once this mastery was achieved, then one was free to abandon oneself to Chan enlightenment and artistic expression. There was no need for the conscious seeking or artistic skill. Only the spontaneous brushwork of the liberated hand and mind was important.

To stress further the distance from artificiality and conscious artistry, Su Dongpo invoked the image of the dream, for:

---

[36] Trans. in Susan Bush, *The Chinese Literati on Painting: Su Shih (1037–1101) to T'ung Ch'i-ch'ang (1555–1636)* (Cambridge, MA: Harvard University Press, 1971), 36.

> What is divinely imparted in a dream is retained by his mind;
> When he awakes he relies on his hand forgetting brush technique.[37]

The artist forgot the conscious artistry of the brush, and relied on his hand to spontaneously express the essence that was retained in his mind.

Su Dongpo wrote about his older contemporary Wen Tong (1018–79), who was well versed in the art of ink paintings depicting bamboo:

> Thus, in painting bamboo one must first have the perfected bamboo in mind. When one takes up the brush and gazes intently, one sees what one wants to paint. Then one rises hurriedly and wields the brush to capture what one sees. It is like the hare's leaping up and the falcon's swooping down; if there is the slightest slackening, then the chance is gone. [Wen Tong] taught me in this way, and I could not achieve it but understood the way it should be done.
>
> Now if one knows the way things should be and cannot do it, inner and outer are not one, mind and hand are not in accord. It is a fault stemming from lack of studying. In other words, the reason why one may see things in the mind, but be awkward in executing them, is that what one sees clearly in everyday life is suddenly lost when it comes to putting it into practice. Does this apply only to bamboo?[38]

This unconscious unity of inner and outer, of hand and mind, is thus necessary for the expression of the living essence of things. The whole process may be described as a forgetting of conceptualization, whether verbal or artistic, and direct confrontation with the essence of things. Then all distinctions will be wiped away in a fusion of self and object; the artist will be so completely involved in the essence of what he is painting that he will become the object itself.

Invoking his favourite philosopher Zhuangzi, Su Dongpo once wrote a poem on a bamboo painting by Wen Tong:

> When Yuke [Wen Tong] painted-bamboo,
> He saw bamboo, not himself.
> Nor was he simply unconscious of himself;
> Trance-like, he left his body.
> His body was transformed into bamboo.

---

[37] Ibid., 36.
[38] Ibid., 37.

Creating inexhaustible freshness.
⌈Zhuangzi⌉ is no longer in this world.
So who can understand such concentration?[39]

According to Su Dongpo, having become the object he is painting, the scholar-painter can now far surpass the mere artisan:

> The artisan of the world may be able to create the forms perfectly, but when it comes to the lightness, unless one is a superior man of outstanding talent one cannot achieve it. In bamboo and rocks, and leafless trees, ⌈Wen Tong⌉ can truly be said to have grasped their way of being: now they are alive and now dead, now twisted and cramped, and now regular and luxuriant. In the roots and stems, joints and leaves, in what is sharp and pointed or veined and striated, there are innumerable changes and transformations never once repeated; yet each part fits in its place, and is in harmony with divine creation and accords with men's conceptions. Is it not because of what the emancipated scholar has lodged in it?[40]

A Broken Branch of Bamboo, attributed to Wen Tong and now in the National Palace Museum (Figure 6.7), exemplifies the art of Wen Tong in which the mind and the brush become inseparable.

The German art historian Roger Goepper has written of this painting:

> All the elements of the plant have been drawn with a single confident brush stroke: the sections of the stem and the branches with a firm and elastic writing brush, the counter-pressure of whose springy tip can be felt in the hand; the leaves with a softer and limper brush, which submits obediently to the slightest pressure of the hand. The interaction of the graphic forms resulting from these two techniques largely determine the general impression created by the painting, the individual elements becoming fused in a composition filled with tension and vitality. The diagonal upward movement of the stem is answered contrapuntally by the smaller twigs, while the sudden break diverts the thrust from the top left-hand corner and causes it to fade out into the largest blank space in the composition.[41]

In perceiving the *li* ('principle') of things (a word that was to become even more important as Neo-Confucianism emerged), Wen Tong might be said to

---

[39] Ibid., 41.
[40] Ibid., 42.
[41] Goepper, *The Essence of Chinese Painting*, 134.

FIGURE 6.7. Wen Tong, *A Broken Branch of Bamboo*, Taipei. From Gugong Shuhua Tulu (Taipei: National Palace Museum, 1991).

be perceiving the essence of things. Here the artist's vocabulary differs from that of the Chan masters, but the underlying thought structure is strikingly similar. Unlike the idea of conventional painting in the Western sense, where a certain distance remains between the painter and the object and the painter remains in control of the painted image, the new *wenren* painting finds the object controlling the painter. The object takes on a life of its own.

To achieve beauty in a work of art and happiness in life, the key is to attain spontaneity. As Su Dongpo observed of his own creative writing such as poetry and prose:

> My writing is like a thousand-gallon spring that issues forth without choosing a site. On level ground it flows smoothly and calmly and can go [a] thousand miles in a day with no trouble. When it twists and winds in the midst of mountains, its appearance changes with the setting, and there is no knowing how it will take shape. But there is one thing I am sure of: it goes when it should go and stops when it has to stop. As for the rest, even I cannot understand it.[42]

[42] Bush, *The Chinese Literati on Painting*, 35.

Finally, with this accent on spontaneity and lack of conscious skill, the traditional models are no longer of prime importance, everything must have a life of its own that is independent of the past. There are two important implications in this for art itself. First, with the brush skill that comes from the practice of calligraphy being the basis of the new *wenren* painting, subjects tend to be those that are open to calligraphic techniques. Consequently, bamboo, rocks, pines and orchids became important. At the same time, pictorial organization had to be held to an absolute minimum. Simplicity was the key word. The conscious skill needed in organizing larger pictures and vistas was both absent and foreign to the idea of natural spontaneity. Furthermore, as pictorial ambition increased, the pictures tended, except in the hands of a few supreme masters, to disintegrate into pieces that have no larger visual integration or unity.

A direct heir to the *yipin* tradition can be found in Liang Kai of the thirteenth century. The immortal or sage in a painting by Liang Kai (Figure 6.8) rambles smilingly and drunkenly. Several quick swipes of ink (in what is usually called 'splashed-ink' [*pomo*] technique) sketch out the figure from shoulder to feet while revealing his inner spirit; they incorporate the soul of the painted figures and the spirits of ardent viewers in all ages. This painting exemplifies Su Dongpo's argument that 'if anyone discusses painting in terms of formal likeness, His understanding is nearly that of a child'.[43] In the West, both Classical Antiquity and Renaissance culture considered that art possessed an essentially illusionist nature; Michelangelo is described as angrily hitting his *Moses* because the statue would not talk or move. Chinese literati were more interested in art's capacity to summon reality and to enter a communion with nature. Some modern Western artists, through intuition, arrived at a conclusion similar to that of the Chinese. Picasso once said to Malraux, 'You're the Chinese one, you know Chinese proverbs. There's one that says the best thing ever said about painting: one must not imitate life, one must work like it.'[44]

---

[43] Ibid., 26.

[44] Quoted in Francois Julien, *The Great Image Has No Form, or On the Nonobject through Painting*, trans. Jane Marie Todd (Chicago: University of Chicago Press, 2009), 239.

FIGURE 6.8. Liang Kai, *Immortal*, Taipei. From Gugong Shuhua Tulu (Taipei: National Palace Museum, 1991).

We can see a continuance of this tradition in the present century in an ink painting (Figure 6.9) by Gao Xingjian, who received the Nobel Prize for literature in 2000 after he left China for self-imposed exile in France. He is also an accomplished painter whose style of ink painting can be

FIGURE 6.9. Gao Xingjian, *Empty Mountain*, Paris. Image reproduced by courtesy of Gao Xingjian.

characterized as belonging to the great Chinese literati tradition of *xieyi* (literally 'writing of the idea').

This style allows him to create subtle, intuitive settings and characters that move in the limits between figurative and abstract art in the same way as many of the Chinese great masters. His paintings explore the expressive possibilities of ink and washes; the nuanced light and dark shadings, subtle washes, textures and volumes in his paintings are both dramatic and refreshing. This painting is Gao Xingjian's interpretation of a poem by the poet–painter Wang Wei (*c.* 700–61). In Gary Snyder's sensitive translation from 1978, the poem reads:

Empty mountains:
>No one to be seen.
Yet – hear –
>human sounds and echoes.
Returning sunlight
>Enters the dark woods;
Again shining
>On the green moss, above.[45]

Gao Xingjian himself wrote about his ink paintings, 'Even when faced with a market choked with trends and fashions, or an environment saturated with political utilitarianism, if the artist is able to remain unmoved, if he does not compromise, then he will be the type of artist who can create a new aesthetic value, and who will continue to write art history.'[46] Gao Xingjian's ink paintings demonstrate that the Chinese literati tradition of achieving beauty through spontaneity, a tradition that was pronounced dead many times by Chinese and foreign critics in the twentieth century, is alive and well.

I should like to conclude with one of the most famous poems in the Chinese tradition. Echoing Zhuangzi's scepticism about the objectivity of beauty, Su Dongpo notes, in a poem about the beautiful and scenic Lu Mountain, the partial condition of our perception, pointing out that one must be content with the immediate awareness of the present moment, of what is – not of what was or will be:

From one side the mountain looks rounded;
From another it is pointed.
Far, near, high, low – no view is the same.
One cannot know the true face of the Lu Mountain;
Only because one is in the mountain.

Beauty and happiness, in the Chinese perspectives outlined above, are like Lu Mountain in its various forms and shapes, to be appreciated by people in their own ways in their existence in the world.

---

[45] Quoted in Eliot Weinberger and Octavio Paz, *Nineteen Ways of Looking at Wang Wei: How a Chinese Poem is Translated* (London: Asphodel Press, 1987), 42.
[46] www.nytimes.com/2008/06/11/arts/11iht-seno.1.13566297.html (accessed 17 June 2009).

7 Terror by beauty: Russo–Soviet perspectives

EVGENY A. DOBRENKO

> Beauty is nothing but the beginning of terror.
>
> *Rainer Maria Rilke*

It is hard to admit, but even talking about beauty is a challenge to the present status quo, as the subject of beauty, which was earlier so urgent and widely discussed (even if it was in an acutely negative context, as, for example, in the era of modernism) and became the basis of an entire discipline – aesthetics – has lost its former popularity. The subject of beauty became unfashionable, even a sign of aesthetic (and political) retrogression. Why did this happen? There was, of course, a tradition, formulated back in the modernist era that linked beauty to the past, and therefore considered an interest in it to be a manifestation of obscurantism. However, another reason that is much later and much more acutely felt by us today is that beauty was inextricably linked to the terrible totalitarian experience of the twentieth century.

This is why many consider it fundamentally blasphemous to use positive aesthetic categories (and the most hallowed among them, beauty) in the description of totalitarian cultures. Poetry, and beauty right along with it, is impossible after Auschwitz. It seems even more impossible, so to speak, *during* Auschwitz. And was it not right of Umberto Eco simply to omit these dark alleyways of twentieth-century history from his landmark anthology *On Beauty: A History of a Western Idea* – which is neither a history of art nor a history of aesthetics but rather an attempt to draw on the histories of both these disciplines to define the ideas of beauty that have informed sensibilities from classical to modern times? Starting with the aesthetic ideal of ancient Greece and ending with the beauty of machines, abstract forms, provocation and consumption, Eco does not even mention 'totalitarian beauty', as if the revival of Beauty and the production of totalitarian kitsch in Nazi Germany, Franco's Spain, Stalinist Russia or Eco's native Italy of 1932 (when he was born) never happened, or as if this painful period of history did not constitute an epicentre of Western history of the twentieth century.[1]

The problem here is purely perceptual. Beauty is always tied to truth, happiness and harmony, and always has a highly positive aura. One cannot deny, however, another important fact: beauty is always tied to art. Art has always been situated close to power (whether sacred or secular). Power is always based on coercion. Hence one might say that coercion is the subconscious of beauty, and beauty is sublimated violence. And in fact, all of aesthetics, as Terry Eagleton has so acutely observed, is 'no more than a name for the political unconscious: it is simply the way social harmony registers itself on our senses, imprints itself on our sensibilities. The beautiful is just political order lived out on the body, the way it strikes the eye and stirs the heart.'[2] Beauty always appeals to harmony, order and law. It has always been thought that the higher the degree of social organization, the more fully the essence of beauty and harmony (as opposed to chaos and anarchy) is manifested in it. And it is no accident that the very idea of beauty developed in the bosom of the Church for centuries. Secularization, however, is tied to democratization, i.e., the disintegration of the existing order. And what comes to replace beauty is the sublime, which Eagleton defines as 'a suitably defused, aestheticized version of the values of the *ancien régime* ... As a kind of terror, the sublime crushes us into admiring submission.'[3]

The twentieth century was one that saw two world wars and terrible terrorist regimes. The rearguard battles of patriarchal societies with the New Age – with individualism, capitalism, progress and political modernization – turned out to be much more terrible and bloodier than the first skirmishes in the nineteenth century. In traditional societies beauty is visible and palpable, and therefore it is indeed the most real legitimization of the *ancien régime*. Using beauty as a cover, traditional societies defend themselves from modernity.

---

[1] See Umberto Eco, *On Beauty: A History of a Western Idea* (London: Secker & Warburg, 2004).

[2] Terry Eagleton, *The Ideology of the Aesthetic* (Oxford: Blackwell, 1990), 37.

[3] Ibid., 54.

What was called beauty in 1930s Europe was in fact the sublime. The concept of the sublime was by no accident the product of the New Age. It is a reaction to the challenge of individualism. The first, most impressive manifestations of this reaction were classicism and romanticism; the difference between them being more stylistic than anything else, since, fundamentally, an identical trauma underlies both, and, therefore, a similar conflict. And it is no coincidence that in the monumental, epic world of Socialist Realism or of Nazism, classicism and romanticism come face to face.

On the whole, aesthetics deals with social trauma. With some intent, Nietzsche called aesthetics 'applied physiology'.[4] Expanding on this idea, Eagleton wrote:

> The aesthetic is … a kind of psychical defense mechanism by which the mind, threatened with an overload of pain, converts the cause of its agony into innocuous illusion. The sublime is therefore the most typical of all aesthetic moods, allowing us as it does to contemplate hostile objects with absolute equanimity, serene in the knowledge that they no longer harm us. In the sublime the paranoid ego fantasizes some state of triumphal invulnerability.[5]

The sublime is always traumatic. It is a desacralized, 'decadent' beauty, one that has become secular and devoid of divine grace. It is an expression of the shock of the individual confronting the Absolute. This is just the variety of the sublime on which romanticism and classicism fed. The totalitarian sublime has a quite different origin: it feeds off the trauma of the collective experience of the patriarchal, culturally immature masses when this experience is shaken by terror. This kind of experience has no internal freedom, since it is completely swallowed up by the interiorization of terror; thus it can produce nothing but a surrogate. Its product is totalitarian kitsch. But a totalitarian regime needs the sublime, not only for the psychological interiorization of its own grandeur by individuals but also to conceal its purely repressive essence.

Beauty is the unarticulated Idea of the Absolute embodied in images. It can only be represented. The sublime, by contrast, is an Idea of the

---

[4] Friedrich Nietzsche, *Nietzsche Contra Wagner, II*, quoted in ibid., 234.
[5] Eagleton, *The Ideology of the Aesthetic*, 163–4.

Absolute that has no representation and cannot be embodied. Any attempt to embody it is deliberately inadequate. Beauty appeals to the ready-made image, while the sublime appeals to the autonomy of subject-ive experience, to individual freedom.[6]

Beauty is tied to ethics: what ethics calls good, art portrays as the beautiful. This is not the case with the sublime, which is so immersed in traumatic experience that it is generally indifferent to ethics. Beauty cannot be conceived without truth: it is a manifestation of truth. But the sublime is indifferent to truth, and harmony is a central problem of aesthetics. Of all the aesthetic categories, it is specifically the sublime that has an active relationship with harmony. If the beautiful is harmony realized, the ugly the impossibility or absence of harmony, the comic lost harmony, and the tragic the death of harmony (or the triumph of disharmony over harmony), then the sublime is the potential possibility of harmony. Within this potentiality lies an active principle, which is lacking in both the beautiful and in the ugly or the tragic. The beautiful (like the tragic) is an established world, while the sublime is a world in the process of formation.

We could also say that the beautiful is the petrified sublime. There are different ways of looking at the relationship between them. Not a few would say that beauty is by far the more elevated, since it appeals to an Absolute, while the sublime is just a conflict between the ideal and the individual, which seeks for perfected forms but fails to find them. There are also many who, on the contrary, suppose that beauty is petrifaction and fetish, while the sublime itself is full of life, emotional experience and exaltation. Be that as it may, beauty in the twentieth century was often turned into a basis for anti-modernist hysterics, or, on the other hand, was a constant target for the modernists' attacks. It is no coincidence that what is posited as new, as a break with tradition, is almost always perceived as a challenge to beauty.

But this is only one aspect of the sublime. Another side of it is a profound internal disharmony. Edmund Burke directly stated that the

---

[6] See Richard Kearney, *The Wake of Imagination: Toward a Postmodern Culture* (London: Routledge, 1994), 175–6; Barnett Newman, 'The Sublime Now', in Charles Harrison and Paul Wood (eds.), *Art in Theory, 1900–1990: An Anthology of Changing Ideas* (Oxford: Blackwell, 1992), 572–4.

source of the sublime is that which is capable of causing suffering or danger, everything that is horrible (and by no means what is beautiful). Therefore we will not err if we say that the source of the sublime is fear. In fact, what we understand as totalitarian beauty is nothing other than sublimated terror. And that is why these images are full of profound trauma. Behind their pompous grandeur, monumental harmony and transcendency lie entropy, violence and a horror of annihilation (as in Burke's famous definition of the sublime: *delightful horror*).[7]

Totalitarian cultures did not know beauty. In their pomposity, monumentalism and megalomania there is not only a political dimension, but also an aesthetic one: the exalted forms of the sublime, passed off as the beautiful. The sublime seeks to pass for the beautiful because precisely what these cultures needed was beauty that would appeal to truth: what is beautiful is true, cannot be false. Hence the enormous legitimizing potential of beauty. In Judaeo-Christian tradition the link between beauty and truth is asserted via a link between beauty and freedom. But something quite different is also true – the obvious connection between beauty and unfreedom.

Let us not forget that even in early-stage so-called utopian socialism, the future society was envisioned as 'harmonized'. In Fourier's futurological schemes this ideal of social harmony found its perceptible embodiment in a 'single architecture'. Remarkably, the 'organized single architecture' in Fourier's projects for the future socialist society acts as a spatial medium that organizes collectivist forms of a harmonious way of life and assures 'splendour' and 'coordination of the whole' of all processes of human vital functions. Here beauty appears in the form of sublimated forcible harmony.

The first dystopian novel in history, which preceded those by George Orwell, Aldous Huxley, Ray Bradbury and others, Evgeny Zamiatin's *We*, begins with this remarkable diary entry by the hero:

> Ballet. Quadratic Harmony ... Why is it beautiful? Why is the dance beautiful? The answer: because it is *unfree* movement, because the entire profound meaning of the dance lies precisely in its absolute, aesthetic subordination, ideal *non-freedom*. And if it's true that our ancestors gave

---

[7] Edmund Burke, *On Taste, on the Sublime and Beautiful: On the French Revolution* (New York: Collier, 1909), 114.

themselves up to dance at the most inspired moments of their lives
(religious mysteries, military parades), then that means only one thing:
the instinct of unfreedom has been organically inherent in man from
ancient times.[8]

Hans Günther points out that in the process of creating a harmonized
nation, all dictatorships realized the cult of beauty in five basic forms:
theatricalization, sacralization, mythologicalization, the production of
visual super-reality and, finally, in the project itself of creating a 'new
person'.[9] I would like to address, however, what made these cultures
different in the way they realized this cult of social harmonization.

That beauty acquired different forms in the different dictatorships
is beyond doubt. In Soviet Russia, for example, which lagged behind
Western civilization with respect to technology, the collision between
patriarchal culture and this Western civilization was so extreme that it gave
rise to the most radical forms of industrial avant-garde art – a complete
rejection of beauty. After the revolution in Russia, 'productionism' arose – a
rejection of beauty in the name of utility. In the Russian avant-garde
we see a rejection of easel painting in favour of industrial design, a rejection
of melodrama in theatre and film and a consolidation of cinematographic
documentalist practice, a rejection of epic tradition in favour of smaller
forms in literature, and functionalism and rationalism in architecture.
French Cubists, German Dadaists and Italian Futurists all, of course,
proclaimed the destruction of beauty. But the extreme radicalism of the
Russian rejection of beauty is tied to the uniqueness of the Russian situation:
as opposed to the West, modernization here was introduced from outside
in the middle of the nineteenth century, and it collided with a deeply
patriarchal culture. The gap between the Westernized modernist project
and patriarchal reality was shocking, and the population's unreadiness for
it was enormous.

Radical tendencies favouring the destruction of beauty had appeared
even earlier. The masses of Savonarola supporters, for example, tore
down statues and destroyed paintings by Florentine masters in the name

---

[8] Yevgeny Zamayatin, *We*, trans. Hugh Aplin (London: Hesperus, 2009), 6.
[9] See Khans Giunter, 'O krasote, kotoraia ne smogla spasti sotsializm', *Novoe
literaturnoe obozrenie*, 101 (2010), 15–16.

of purifying a true divine beauty. But the very same could be said of twentieth-century modernist art, in which iconoclasm was part of the struggle against beauty as it was traditionally understood. Essentially, modernism is nothing but a revolt against the former ideal of beauty. Aesthetic nihilism in Russia had taken shape by the end of the nineteenth century, and after the revolution it could be found everywhere. In 1931 the critic Nikolai Iezuitov wrote, in his article 'The End of Beauty': 'The heroism of socialist labour and beauty are incompatible concepts ... To call our socialist construction beautiful is cynicism in regard to the construction and militant work of the proletariat.'[10] The proletarian poet Vladimir Kirillov defiantly wrote, 'for the sake of our tomorrow, we will burn Raphael, tear down the museums, and trample the flowers of art. We breathe a different kind of beauty'. He was echoed by the Russian Revolution's main poet, Vladimir Mayakovsky: 'It's time to riddle the museum walls with bullets.' But even as Leon Trotsky criticized the radicalism of the avant-garde, he was already asserting that 'the grand style of the future will not be decorative, but formative. The Futurists are right about this.'[11]

The avant-garde's iconoclasm, its fight against mimetic art, easel painting, and realistic figurativeness were what Stalinism rejected. Something similar is known in the history of Christianity. Iconoclasm arose, as is well known, in the first millennium (especially in the sixth and seventh centuries). Nevertheless, a return to representation also occurred. This was occasioned by the appearance of the *Biblia pauperum* in the later Middle Ages. In fact, one of the main arguments in favour of representational art, and the basis of the artistic tradition of the Western world, was as a positive solution to the question of accessibility to scripture for those who did not know how to read (who constituted the overwhelming majority of the population). Indeed, thanks to medieval Christian art and the humanist resurrection of Greek and Roman art, we now possess a single artistic language. Furthermore, it is in just this language and in this tradition that the historical code for expressing and reproducing the common concepts of our understanding of self is to be found. At the end of the eighteenth century this code was abruptly shattered.

[10] N. Iezuitov, 'Konets krasote', *Proletarskaia literatura*, 4 (1931), 158.
[11] Lev Trotsky, *Literatura i revoliutsiia* (Moscow: Politizdat, 1991), 192.

The religion of the New Age is democratization. It led to profound political implications, as well as aesthetic ones. The democratization of patriarchal societies is a complex and dangerous process, since these societies are often not only unprepared for liberalization but often actively oppose it. In this respect, the breakdown into a 'new Middle Ages' in the twentieth century was no accident. Each mobilizational regime saw itself not as a continuation of history but as a corrective of it. Fundamental to each is a rejection of the course of the historical process that aims at secularization, modernization, individualism, and the rejection of patriarchal values and the peasant way of life. These regimes attempted to turn history backwards, and therefore they referenced Antiquity: it allowed them to skip over the detested liberal–bourgeois period as if starting all over again, and simultaneously it guaranteed continuity.

Since the twentieth century was the century of the cult of progress, all of the totalitarianisms that grew out of revolutions and wars positioned themselves as progressive, oriented toward the future and to ideas of national revival. Hitler constructed his thousand-year Reich; the Soviet Union laid a path for humanity to the bright world of eternal communism. These regimes rushed towards economic modernization. The main thing that made them alike was the answer to the question of the value and the boundaries of modernizing projects. In them, the price paid for economic modernization was political conservation, the social status quo and a historical *revanche*. Essentially, these regimes were oriented not to the future but to the past. Modernizations in them were realized in the name of preservation of or a return to a pre-capitalist, peasant/patriarchal and feudal/militaristic past. Paradoxically, modernization was not supposed to let the future come, but rather to preserve the past. It was supposed to stave off the danger of internationalism, cosmopolitanism, liberalism, personalism, the values of a democratic political culture based not on force but on social compromises, cultural diversity, political pluralism and the spirit of free criticism – all of the things that inevitably destroy these nationalist/isolationist, conservative/patriarchal, tribal, communal/hierarchical, militaristic/mobilizational and aggressive regimes based on violence.

Having gone backwards, they took even their aesthetic ideals from the past. Thus, at the heart of these societies lies the idea of retardation, preservation rather than transformation of the patriarchal order. Hence the orientation to exemplars from the past. At the ideological level this type of society relies on 'priestly' rather than legal practices, on morality rather than law, and on faith rather than rationality. Hence the reliance on a mystical principle, on the sublime passed off as beauty.

If for the modernists beauty was the future, then for totalitarian regimes such beauty was the present, to the degree that it drew its inspiration from the past. In the name of traditional beauty, Nazi culture rejected 'degenerative' modernism, and Stalinism fought against 'formalism' and explained to Shostakovich and Eisenstein that the language of art must be simple and accessible to the broad masses. Both campaigns were in fact running in parallel in 1936 and 1937, at the height of the Great Terror in the USSR.

Stalinism rejected rationalism and functionalism in favour of an exuberant baroque, an exaltation of formal decorations. Its forms and stylizations modelled the patriarchal imaginary and were the embodiment of the archetype of the ideal dwelling of yesterday's peasant. Stalinism appeals not so much to rational forms as to the forms of the 'tsarist tower' that struck the peasants pouring into the cities in the 1920s and 1930s: Empire style, the church, and the decorations of rich interiors. The masses in Germany and, even more so, those in Italy did not experience such a culture shock, since they lived in a completely different visual milieu.

In Stalinism this hinged on a no less radical appeal to an ancient ideal of beauty – specifically, to Greece and Rome. Never mind that practically all the European dictatorships harked back to them: Stalinism reproduced this ideal stylistically in the most consistent way. In Abram Room's 1934 film *A Strict Youth*, discussions about the new socialist morality take place in the stadium, as if brought directly from Greece and Rome into the Soviet Union. Even the poses that the characters assume are 'Greek'.

In the Stalinist era, Soviet reality is represented as a conflict-free idyll in which 'beautiful relationships among people' prevail and 'the beautiful is born every day and every hour in the life itself of Soviet society'.[12] Art is only a reflection of the beauty of the Soviet life.

[12] V. Ermilov, 'Za boevuiu teoriiu literatury! Prekrasnoe – eto nasha zhizn', *Literaturnaia gazeta* (17 November 1948).

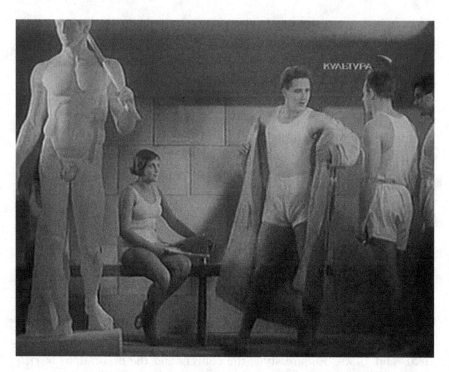

FIGURE 7.1. Still from Abram Room's film *A Strict Youth* (1934).

Generally speaking, the rejection of utility in favour of self-sufficient beauty reaches no less a degree of radicalization in Stalinist culture than the productionism that had preceded it in the rejection of beauty in favour of utility. Everything 'ugly', for example, is removed from the streets – public toilets, kiosks, public counters. Not only does life make way for beauty, life itself becomes an ornament alongside the endless porticoes, pilasters and capitals. Here is what one of the leading Stalinist architects, Ivan Zholtovsky, had to say about this: 'The rhythm and motion of the main-artery streets should be maintained by intervals between individual buildings. These intervals must not be empty, they must be executed artistically. Something beautiful should be seen in these intervals: children strolling through greenery, flowering bushes and lawns, fountains, and trees.'[13]

---

[13] *Mastera sovetskoi arkhitektury ob arkhitekture*, vol. I (Moscow: Iskusstvo, 1975), 42.

In Germany the rejection of traditional beauty in Dadaism and Expressionism was motivated by a completely different reason: the unwillingness of the artistic elites to stay within the paradigm of 'bourgeois beauty'. The modernist impulse had a different basis from that in Russia. This is why the Nazi rejection of 'degenerative art' was interpreted as a return to 'folk culture' that was designed with a myth of 'blood and soil' as a point of departure. Stylistically, this was formulated with reference to Rome but with a strong Nordic component that was not present in Stalinism. There is a clear difference between Stalinist baroque and the restrained Nazi Empire style.

The difference is even more obvious when comparing the two main architectural projects of Nazi Germany and Stalinist Russia: the Germania Project in Berlin and the Palace of the Soviets in Moscow. Of course, with respect to the people-less urbanist beauty that is easily seen from an aeroplane, but which only the masses – not individuals – can inhabit, the twentieth century surpassed all foregoing eras. Megalomania unites these two projects. The Germania Project – the creation of a new capital for the thousand-year Reich in place of Berlin – included the highest cupola in the world, alongside which the Brandenburg Gate (and for that matter, all of old Berlin) would seem like a grain of sand. The Stalinist Palace of the Soviets was conceived as the tallest building in the world. On top of the palace a 120-metre statue of Lenin was to be erected. This pinnacle of Stalinist megalomania was supposed to be a palace for the people, combining the pomposity of the Egyptian pyramids, the grandeur of ancient Rome and the sanctity of temple architecture. The Palace of the Soviets is an example of the use of traditional sacred images of beauty for secular (political) purposes. It was to stand on the site of Moscow's largest cathedral, which was demolished in 1931.

These projects are similar in their megalomania. However, serious stylistic differences begin to appear, and are especially obvious when one compares the art of Stalinism, Nazism and Italian Fascism. Futurism was still an officially recognized art in painting, and the so-called Rationalist–Fascist style was dominant in Italian architecture.[14] This latter was far

---

[14] See Borden Painter, *Mussolini's Rome: Rebuilding the Eternal City* (Basingstoke: Palgrave Macmillan, 2005).

FIGURE 7.2. Albert Speer, Germania Project.

removed from ancient Rome's exemplars of beauty, and in fact relied on constructivism. Why? Mainly because the broad masses in Italy (as opposed to those in Russia) lived in an environment of Classical beauty, and therefore revolutionary culture suggested something different to them. For the Soviet masses, a tsar's palace was the equivalent, but for the Italians it was constructivism that removed the decorative element from the Classical beauty surrounding them. In Germany the references to ancient Rome were combined with constructivist severity.[15] But in Russia, Empire style was represented in an almost baroque style of execution. By contrast, the art of Franco's Spain combined Empire style with Catholic kitsch.

Following on from the preceding, I would argue for the importance of the aesthetic dimension and therefore for taking an aesthetic approach to different totalitarian regimes. We have to evaluate the importance of Stalinist, Nazi and Fascist beauty from a viewpoint of the social trauma

---

[15] See Alex Scobie, *Hitler's State Architecture: The Impact of Classical Antiquity* (University Park: Pennsylvania State University Press, 1990); Robert Taylor, *The Word in Stone: The Role of Architecture in the National Socialist Ideology* (Berkeley and Los Angeles: University of California Press, 1974); Stephen Helmer, *Hitler's Berlin: The Speer Plans for Reshaping the Central City* (Ann Arbor: UMI Research Press, 1980).

condensed in these cultures. In the 1930s these regimes began to isolate themselves from the predominant rationalism with the peculiar, indecipherable language of trauma, and, in the space of utopia, the theatricalization of its traumas was completed.[16] Thus, communism and the 'Thousand-Year Reich' were the imagined total compensation for trauma; this was perhaps the only role that they completely fulfilled. Therefore, we may say that Stalinist, Nazi or Fascist art became a sort of 'pure art'. De-realization of life achieved a truly finished form in it. In this aestheticized world, everything was immersed into such a nirvana of style that consumption of this art might well be compared to the effect of profound anaesthesia. Indeed, the more pain society must endure, the more, and stronger, anaesthetic it needs; that is, the more beautiful life has to become. Ultimately, the ability of Soviet society to endure terror was directly proportional to the *unbearable beauty of Stalinism.*

As Jeffrey Schnapp suggests, any revolutionary culture – Fascist, Nazi or Communist – by its very nature aspires to overcome a social isolation of the culture of the preceding period. Producing new subjects, new citizens and mass societies, modern revolutionary cultures expand by drawing in ever-newer realms. Within such a context the word 'culture' takes on a distinctive set of meanings that run the full spectrum from the resistant to the autonomous to the instrumental. In ways that are fundamentally different in comparison with prior centuries, and that exceed and/or alter the practices characteristic of liberal-democratic regimes, culture matters to dictatorial nation-states because it is accepted as an integral weapon of political rule: as a domain of political symbolization; as the only way to produce a self-image of power; as a means of outreach, co-optation and interpolation of political subjects. Culture under modern dictatorships moves beyond traditional settings such as the court, gallery, salon and theatre, out into public squares, libraries and schools, state institutions, sports arenas and television: the characteristic spaces of industrial mass societies, where an increasingly mature print culture can interact with newer image, voice and communications technologies. Within this expanded public sphere the concept of 'culture' gradually

---

[16] Mikhail Ryklin, *Prostranstva likovaniia: Totalitarizm i razlichie* (Moscow: Logos, 2002), 23.

broadens out to encompass everything from the arts to physical recreation, to ideological training, even hygiene. Its normative audience is increasingly assumed to be the masses: masses that need to be shaped and modernized by 'cultural' means.[17]

The total aestheticization of politics, however, is not by any means tied only to the instrumentalization of aesthetics to strengthen the effectiveness of propaganda, to the creation of a mass society, to the development of technologies, or to severely traumatized societies' rejection of rationalism. It is also linked with the aesthetic nature of the totalitarian state itself.

Mussolini, who defined Fascism as a 'doctrine of power and beauty',[18] once called it 'a glass house'. This was not intended as a comment on architecture but rather on the need for transparency in government. In other words, Mussolini was contrasting his regime with the corruption and confusion of the semi-democracy that had preceded it. But the tradition in Italy, as well as in Russia (communists shared the same sentiments when it comes to what Hitler called plutocracy), was just the opposite: total social corruption. That is why it established a 'direct line' between the leader and the masses: purely transparent with no obstacles. Thus the system operates with this transparent and purely imaginative ideal construction. The ideal artist, writer or architect is someone who delivers a plan and realizes it according to his vision, with no concessions to reality; that is, he holds full authority over reality. In other words, he is the leader. The leader was not simply *represented* as an artist–demiurge (an architect, painter, or poet): he in fact *was* such an artist.[19] In completing the creative act, the artist–demiurge transforms reality by subjugating it to his artistic will. Reality is his raw material, which is harmonized as a result of the creative force exerted by the artist over the material. As a matter of fact, the content of the creative act is precisely in this act of exertion of will, and thus it is congruent to the exercise of political will.

---

[17] Jeffrey Schnapp's Keynote speech 'How to Conceptualise Culture Under a Dictatorship' at the conference 'Mapping and Framing Cultural Spaces Under a Dictatorship' (University of Manchester, 5 Dec. 2008). See also Jeffrey Schnapp, 'Fascinating Fascism', *Journal of Contemporary History*, 31/2, Special Issue: The Aesthetics of Fascism (April 1996), 235–44.

[18] Simonetta Falasca-Zamponi, *Fascist Spectacle: The Aesthetics of Power in Mussolini's Italy* (Berkeley: University of California Press, 1997), 16.

[19] See Éric Michaud, *The Cult of Art in Nazi Germany*, trans. Janet Lloyd (Stanford, CA: Stanford University Press, 2004).

The status itself of the figure of the leader has an extraordinary significance in totalitarian cultures. In Soviet culture this aspect is particularly interesting: in contrast to Fascist Italy or Nazi Germany, where the cult of the leader was an integral part of the official ideology and was therefore explicitly articulated, the 'cult of personality' in the Soviet Union was officially condemned because it did not comply with the Marxist ideology of emphasizing the social over the individual. Stalin's cult was passed off as a 'spontaneous' demonstration of the love of the people for the great leader.[20] Thus, in the Soviet Union the leader was proclaimed to be the embodiment of 'the objectively beautiful'. In an important 1950 article entitled 'On the Problem of the Beautiful in Soviet Art', the Soviet critic German Nedoshivin stated: 'Amid all the wealth of the beautiful material of life, the first place is held by the images of our great leaders Lenin and Stalin. The sublime beauty of the images of the leaders of all the people ... is the basis for the confluence of "the beautiful" and "the true" in the art of socialist realism.'[21]

If we compare the visual renderings of the leader's image in different totalitarian cultures we see that the unrealized sexual fantasies of the masses are transferred onto the leader (the Führer, Il Duce, El Caudillo); the structure of the patriarchal authoritarian family facilitates this displacement. As Wilhelm Reich demonstrated in *The Mass Psychology of Fascism* as long ago as 1933, this is precisely the source of the 'national narcissism' that sublimates the emotional enslavement of an individual into the cult of 'nation' (and, in Soviet Russia, the cult of a hegemonic class). As parts of a great collective, the representatives of the masses attempt to compensate for their difficult material conditions:

> The more helpless a 'mass individual' becomes (owing to his upbringing), the more distinctly his identification with the Führer is evidenced, and the more deeply his childish need for protection is concealed in his feeling of oneness with the Führer ... The horror of his material and sexual situation is so overshadowed by the exalted idea of his belonging to the

20 See Jan Plamper, *The Stalin Cult: A Study of the Alchemy of Power* (New Haven: Yale University Press, 2012).

21 German Nedoshivin, *Voprosy teorii sovetskogo izobrazitel'nogo iskusstva* (Moscow: Akademiia khudozhestv SSSR, 1950), 92.

race of gentlemen, the existence of an outstanding Führer, that in time he completely loses the concept of the whole insignificance of his blind dedication.[22]

Reich said in 1933 what did not become a commonplace until the late twentieth century: the masses unknowingly wanted Fascism (and, one might add, Stalinism and the other dictatorships that ruled the world in the last century and continue to rule it in the twenty-first); this order could not have been imposed upon them against their will. The aggressive potential of the masses in crisis situations is enormous, the frustration of the masses with their inability to adequately respond to the challenges of modernization limitless, and the leader simply reveals them and, through the institutions of power, directs and realizes them. Fascism, Stalinism and Nazism are all primarily the problem of the masses, and not of Hitler, Stalin, Mussolini, Mao Zedong, Kim Il-sung or Pol Pot (the list might be lengthened by many other names of currently active political figures).

Beauty is linked with sacrality. But although all these regimes had very different relationships to God and were often based on theomachism, iconoclasm and atheism, in actuality they were not, of course, essentially secular. It was no coincidence that they always made reference to the people and to popular spirit, as they saw in them either an expression of ideals or of the progressive class (in the Soviet case), or as a higher race (in the Nazi case), or as the defenders of the nation (the Italian case), or as the exponents of traditional patriarchal and Catholic virtues (Franco's Spain and Salazar's Portugal).

In this respect Stalinist culture is particularly interesting, since it could allow itself to officially proclaim atheism while nonetheless preserving all the attributes of sacrality in the cult of leaders. Why could this happen in Soviet Russia? Because, being completely demiurgic, it simply duplicated the sacrality in itself – it had no need of an external God. Everything that these cultures present is a beatified image of the common people. The people are the definitive referent of terror. They are the source of terror, which is simply formulated ideologically and

---

[22] Wilhelm Reich, *The Mass Psychology of Fascism*, trans. Vincent Carfagno (Harmondsworth: Penguin, 1975), 85.

institutionalized politically by the reigning power. 'The people' are, in fact, the mouthpiece of the ultimate will, and therefore they become a subject equal to God. Or, rather, they cease to need God. For this reason they stop being Godfearing and themselves become the only object of the cult.

As Mikhail Ryklin observes, the atheism of a terror that relies on collective bodies and includes God in itself in the form of a people is 'the atheism of a new religion capable of feeding a social life based on coercion with itself'.[23] Art imposes upon us much more profound, even archetypical, notions of the greatness of the people than a simple visual image. Furthermore, without art this 'people' cannot be created. Just as a church is an institution for maintaining and promoting a religious cult, totalitarian regimes are institutions for maintaining and promoting the cult of the patriarchal masses. Totalitarian dictatorships engage in the production of collective bodies. Totalitarian art is the production of collective identity. Accordingly, it is one of the basic elements of these regimes, no less important than the KGB, the Gestapo, or the Gulag. Essentially, art takes the place of the Church. Hence, as we have seen, these cultures manifest a special status for the shaping of public spaces; thus also the reliance on convention in the form of traditional beauty, transformed and sublimated, and on the collective identity rather than on the personality of the artist.

This last aspect causes real drama in creative work. Beauty is canon. In this sense, it is a source of terror for the artist, the chief danger for whom is that of self-expression in the face of beauty. It is a mortal danger. Under such conditions, 'culture becomes possible in the form of aggression against culture', as Ryklin states, defining the possibilities of functioning of the 'ecstatic culture'.[24] This culture always harks back to folklore and the epic canon, in which not only the ontological irrationality of these cultures but also their genealogy are manifested. Their references to the land and fertility, and to blood and soil, reveal the peasant origin of what is imagined by the new proletarianized urban masses, who, although they have been subjected to urbanization, have continued to

---

[23] Mikhail Ryklin, *Terrorologiki* (Tartu-Moscow: Ad Marginem, 1992), 214.
[24] Ibid., 85.

FIGURE 7.3. Boris Iofan, Palace of the Soviets.

see themselves in a specifically folkloric context. To interiorize terror, these masses need the primordial beauty of an epic.[25]

Striking in Soviet painting are the pictures that portray a total exultation that is inseparable from the land and fertility. In these pictures, one can read the genealogy of the gaze in Stalinist culture. We are confronted by a pure exemplar of the sublime: 'these masses see only in the pitch dark of the nonexistent; that is, they see not what is, but only their own unrealized possibilities. It is just these possibilities that block in these collective bodies the vision of themselves as the bodies to which something is happening.'[26]

Another point of reference, as we have seen, is Classical Antiquity. Its visual representations are in architecture. In its reliance on the people,

[25] Ibid.
[26] Ibid., 42.

FIGURE 7.4. Arkadii Plastov, *Harvest Festival* (1938). © 2013, State Russian Museum, St Petersburg.

Stalinist architecture harks back to the exemplars of folk art. This is particularly evident in the All-Union Agricultural Exhibition (1939), wherein the pavilions combine images of abundant fruit, femininity, fertility, a surplus of agricultural products and an abundance of fountains. The exhibition was described as an exemplar of beauty. It was itself a work of art and brought realized socialism *together* with beauty. In identifying with his own image in the exhibition, the spectator was himself 'adorned', since, as a reviewer wrote, 'an important feature of the exhibition is that the achievements in the area of agriculture and industry are directly tied in the conscience of the Soviet people to a sense of the beauty of what they have made with their own hands'.[27] But this is an esoteric beauty. It was, as was said then, a 'reflection' of reality that simultaneously bore within itself some kind of light that was invisible to ordinary vision. As another reviewer wrote, everyone tried to 'reflect the beauty of our socialist reality'; but, he asked himself, 'Do all the objects in the exhibition bear these features of the new beauty? Of course, not all to the same degree, but in almost every element of the equipment – be

[27] V. Tolstoi, 'Leninskii plan monumental'noi propagandy v deistvii', *Iskusstvo*, 1 (1952), 60.

FIGURE 7.5. Boris Yakovlev, *Dispute about Art* (1946). © 2013, State Russian Museum, St Petersburg.

it a chandelier, a rug, a stained-glass window, an ornament, the vases, a stand [and one could add: frescoes, majolica, mosaics, carvings, etc.] – this spark of the truly visible beauty of our life shines through.'[28]

If all this beauty was hand-made, then the beauty of the female body in its natural state might be considered the best stylistic indicator. The woman in Soviet painting is always represented as the embodiment of quietness, simplicity and joyful labour, which is especially emphasized when she is styled after ancient models. Female nudity is so rare here that it even became a subject of discussion in Boris Yakovlev's painting *Dispute about Art* (1946): against a backdrop of revolutionary and battle canvases, an almost Rubenesque Diana is depicted.

---

[28] A. Zhukov, 'Arkhitekturno-planirovochnyi ansambl' Vsesoiuznoi sel'skokhoziaistvennoi vystavki', *Arkhitektura SSSR*, 7 (1954), 14.

In Nazi painting the woman is presented in a completely different way; in that culture there is exaltation and sensuality. But specifically because the Soviet woman is portrayed much more 'realistically' in Soviet visual art, the evolution of the Soviet ideal of beauty is quite apparent in the history of the change in female images. In revolution-era posters women were portrayed as revolutionaries and soldiers, and often these images were created through montage. In the First Five-Year Plan era, the images were primarily of working women, and in the latter 1930s female images were athletic, healthy. However, by the time of late Stalinism we see a woman in a commercial poster that reflects the post-war Stalinist style of luxury. The austerity of revolutionary times has passed and has been replaced with 'new' bourgeois values. The woman is no longer presented as a model of proletarian humility: she drinks – far from proletarian – champagne from an elegant 'bourgeois' crystal wineglass, and in front of her are the fruits of the south – grapes. Or else she is busy with such feminine things as buying beautiful fabrics, which was completely alien to the way the Soviet woman was depicted in revolution: at labour, looking rather more like a man. Petty-bourgeois beauty became a 'luxury' and permeated Soviet everyday life as it was officially presented.

As opposed to the other European totalitarian dictatorships, Stalinism lasted a long time and died very slowly. One cannot say that it is quite dead in present-day Russia, where the political culture remains etatist and nationalist, there remains a repressive police state, and power is concentrated in the hands of an authoritarian leader. Perhaps this is why Stalinism alone produced a reflexive tendency in art, a curious postmodern wonderland. Two Moscow conceptual artists, Vitaly Komar and Alexander Melamid, emigrated to the USA in the 1970s, where they created a new style called Sots Art (following the example of Pop art). This style parodies Soviet political imagery, subverting and taking it to a level of absurdity. Curiously, the main thing reflected in their Nostalgic Socialist Realism series is precisely the beauty of Stalinist Empire style. In the pictures *Stalin and Muses* and *The Birth of Socialist Realism* Stalin figures in a classicist setting, surrounded by ancient goddesses.

In *View of the Kremlin in a Romantic Landscape*, a red curtain is held open by unseen hands to reveal a Poussinesque landscape complete with ruins

FIGURE 7.6. Poster, *Liberated Woman – Build up Socialism!* by Adolf Iosifovich Strakhov-Braslavsky. State History Museum, Moscow. © Museum Stock (1926).

FIGURE 7.7. Poster, *Soviet Champagne: Best Grape Vine* Martinov, N. I.
(1952). Image courtesy of Soviet Art Me.

FIGURE 7.8. Vitaliy Komar and Alexander Melamid, *Stalin and Muses.*
Image courtesy of Vitaly Komar.

FIGURE 7.9. Vitaliy Komar and Alexander Melamid, *The Birth of Socialist Realism* (1982–3). Image courtesy of Vitaly Komar.

(as if the Soviet empire has become the new/ancient Rome) and the Kremlin floating like a fairy-tale castle on an island in an azure sea. Traditional beauty visualizes the traumatic experience of unrealized Soviet greatness, producing quasi-futuristic and simultaneously nostalgic post-Soviet phantasmagoria.

Komar and Melamid have shown, in fact, that beauty is merely a form of terror. And there is a profound truth in this: Beauty *is* form. Not by chance do we see this in the Latin *formosus* (beautiful) and *formositas* (beauty). On the other hand, since the times of the actual founder of modern aesthetics, Kant, beauty has been contraposed to utility. The beautiful is that which is not useful, and the useful that which is not beautiful. Beauty is self-sufficient, while utility is only a means, and cannot be an end in itself – its purpose lies outside it. In this respect, totalitarian regimes do not really know beauty. They only know it in the form of the sublime.

Dostoyevsky asserted that beauty will save the world. The history of the twentieth century, in which political beauty dominated – that is, there was simply no distinction between beauty and utility – does not inspire optimism. But let us make no mistake: beauty is inseparable from political utility in the same way that religion is inseparable from politics. That is why the politicization of beauty and the beautification (i.e. aestheticization) of politics in the twentieth century were the response to the total social secularization of the New Age. We must not forget either, however, that this is a purely Western phenomenon. In obscurantist societies, in traditional Eastern forms of despotism, wherein religion successfully opposes secularity, religion specifically is the driving and legitimizing force of politics. Therefore it would be correct to say that beauty, along with religion, is only one of the functions of the spiritual essence of mankind. Both of them refer to a utopia of collective salvation. Beauty is the paradise lost of the New Age person. In order to 'save the world', beauty must emerge from the shadow of the sublime; that is, it must again become a religion. The price of salvation for the European in this case would be a return to the Middle Ages.

8 The science and beauty of nebulae

CAROLIN CRAWFORD

Spectacular astronomical images of clusters of blue stars deeply embedded in vibrant clouds of dusty gas have become abundant over the last decade. Collected using space telescopes and a new generation of ground-based instruments, these pictures awe us with their glorious landscapes of multi-coloured gas sculpted to form swirls and filaments. Black misshapen blobs and tenuous drifts of dust are seen in silhouette against the glow of the gas, and the whole is peppered with aggregations of brilliant, bright blue stars. Many of these vistas are by now familiar to the layperson (for example, the 'pillars of creation' shown in Figure 8.1), who is able to appreciate their beauty without necessarily requiring comprehension of what is being portrayed. In this chapter I shall revisit such images with the aim of deconstructing them in order to explain the science that underlies the beauty.

The interstellar medium

We live in a spiral galaxy, flattened out to form a giant frisbee slowly wheeling in space, with our own Sun just one of two hundred thousand million stars all bound together by their mutual gravity. A central bulge of stars is surrounded by an extended flat disc that contains the spiral arms, which are traced by conspicuous clusters of young blue stars (see the Whirlpool Galaxy, shown in Figure 8.2). We live within such a spiral arm, about halfway from the centre to the edge of our own galaxy, the Milky Way. The clusters of stars most apparent in our night sky – such as the Pleiades, or the double star cluster in Perseus – are prominent because they are physically close to us, located in neighbouring spiral arms. As we will learn later, blue stars such as those seen in these clusters are hot, massive, and the most recently formed. But whilst they are the

FIGURE 8.1. The 'pillars of creation' in the Eagle Nebula. Long towers of interstellar gas and dust emerge from the walls of the Eagle Nebula seen in silhouette against the glow of background emission. For colour images of the figures appearing in this chapter, see www.darwin.cam.ac.uk/lectures/beauty.
Credit: NASA, ESA, STScI, J. Hester and P. Scowen (Arizona State University).

most obvious feature to draw the eye and delineate the structure, a galaxy does not consist solely of stars. It is easy to dismiss the void between the stars as being only empty space; even though it might be millions of times emptier than the best vacuum that we can achieve in a laboratory on Earth, it is not completely devoid of matter. Interstellar space abounds with atoms and molecules of gas, alongside tiny solid particles that we

FIGURE 8.2. The 'Whirlpool' spiral galaxy. Our face-on view of the disc of the 'Whirlpool' spiral galaxy clearly shows the spiral arms delineated by bright blue star clusters, pink emission nebula and dark obscuring dust lanes.
Credit: NASA, ESA, S. Beckwith (STScI), and the Hubble Heritage Team (STScI/ AURA).

refer to as 'dust'. This material is very sparsely distributed – perhaps only a few dozen atoms would be contained in a scoop of space the volume of a can of drink – but a lot of matter can be tucked away within the enormous volumes lying between the stars. This gas and dust comprise what we call the *interstellar medium*.

All the gas within our galaxy has a mass that is only around a tenth of that contained in stars. Most of the gas is primordial hydrogen and helium, formed at the very beginning of the Universe but not yet incorporated into the formation of the stars of our Milky Way. This is mixed with a trace of heavier elements, such as carbon, oxygen and iron, which were cooked up in the interiors of massive stars and then flung out into space when the stars exploded at the ends of their lives. These gas clouds of interstellar matter are of fundamental importance to us all, as they are the reservoir from which new stars are born – along with the planets around those stars and, of course, any life forms living on those planets. It is the interstellar medium that forms the focus for this chapter: a story that concerns not only stars, but also the gaseous clouds that lie in between the stars in space, which are revealed in *nebulae*.

Some of this gas is accommodated in a widespread inter-cloud atmosphere, very sparsely distributed and at temperatures of millions of degrees, so incredibly hot that it cannot be detected other than at X-ray wavelengths. Invisible and transparent at lower energy wavebands, this X-ray gas is not relevant to our discussion. Embedded within the hot atmosphere are far cooler, denser clouds that contain a comparable amount of the mass but inhabit a far smaller volume. Such diffuse cold clouds encompass the entire disc of our galaxy and extend out beyond the visible spiral arms. The gas in these clouds is so cold (at temperatures of tens to hundreds of degrees above absolute zero) that matter is mostly in the form of neutral hydrogen atoms, detectable only in the radio waveband and again transparent to our eyes. But if the neutral atoms are heated by a flood of energetic ultraviolet photons from a nearby young star, they store and re-radiate this energy as light, causing the gas to glow with radiation. It is at this point that the gas clouds become apparent as the distinctive pinky-red nebulae that accompany the blue star clusters lining the spiral arms (Figure 8.2).

An aside on the colours in the images

The only way astronomers can learn about distant cosmic objects out beyond the Solar System is through the light they emit. Everything we know about the stars, nebulae and distant galaxies is inferred from how we analyse and interpret that light. There are many colours of light, each corresponding to a different wavelength. In the optical band, this is easily demonstrated by the way that sunlight can be dispersed into a rainbow using a prism. Beyond this rainbow lie the exotic realms of the infrared, the radio, the ultraviolet and X-ray wavebands, all containing far more colours that are completely undetectable except with specialist telescopes and instruments. All stars such as the Sun emit many colours continuously to give a *spectrum* of colour. Individual atoms contained in a diffuse cloud emit light very differently, however, giving off only very specific colours, each of a particular wavelength.

An atom is composed of a cloud of electrons surrounding a central more massive nucleus; these electrons can only inhabit specific energy levels, like books that are constrained to sit only on shelves in a bookcase. If illuminated by a source of energetic light, an atom can absorb energy and store it by temporarily raising one or more of its electrons to higher energy levels. When the energy is released later in the form of a photon of light, the amount available depends on the difference between the electron energy levels. This in turn is a well-defined quantity, crucially dependent on the atomic structure of that element. Thus the photons liberated by an atom can only have certain energies, which correspond to specific wavelengths. In this way, the colours radiated by gas atoms of each element produce a unique fingerprint, revealed in sharp spikes of colour within a spectrum known as emission lines. Analysis of these lines can tell much about the chemical composition of an emitting cloud, and the details of relative strengths of lines of different colour can inform us about the density and temperature of the gas. The nebulae in images of all galaxies are predominantly a pinky-red, as it is the dominant colour emitted by excited hydrogen, by far and away the most common element in the Universe. Additional colours such as blue and green are produced by atoms of many other common elements, including nitrogen, oxygen, neon and sulphur.

When using images to study astronomical objects, astronomers do not obtain the data with a camera that collects all the light at once. Instead, separate images are taken of the object, each viewed through a succession of filters to isolate specific bands of colour. Wide filters let a broad range of colour through and are used for imaging the stars, which emit colour at a continuous range of wavelengths: the balance of light between red, green and blue wide filters can allow us to distinguish the colours of the stars. Narrow filters are used to isolate specific colours that can trace the light from particular excited atoms within a gas cloud. Most commonly a narrow red filter is used to detail the distribution of the hydrogen present, although many other wavebands are commonly in use. The final image is compiled from matching observations which are usually obtained through a range of both broad and narrow filters, all of which are colourized appropriately before being combined. The variety of colours represented will thus depend on how many different filters were used to form the composite. The simplest details are obtained with a wide blue filter (to pinpoint the blue stars) and a narrow red filter (to map out the accompanying gas cloud); far more complex multi-coloured maps are only possible with long dedicated observations through a whole host of different filters.

Many of the visible-light images that are publicly available have been constructed with a view to faithfully recreating the 'true' colour of the light emitted. The brightness of the diffuse gaseous structures is usually exaggerated, as only short exposures through a wide filter are necessary to bring out the location of bright stars, but much longer exposures are required to include faint wisps of a surrounding nebula. This means that viewing a nebula by eye, even through a very powerful telescope, is far less spectacular than the images might suggest. The mismatch is compounded by the fact that the cells in the retina of the eye that are most sensitive to faint diffuse structures are those that are least responsive to colour. Obviously, images that are collected from other (non-optical) emission, such as the infrared or X-ray, must be portrayed using 'false' colours so we can view them. When such images are accommodated within a visible image for comparative purposes, it can lead to a portrayal that may not be 'true' but is at least accurate in spirit. For example, if an image incorporates near-infrared light, this band would most likely be coloured red, and the colours given to the optical images shifted blueward, retaining an informative and coherent sense of the comparative colour.

Emission nebulae

A typical pink emission nebula in our galaxy is the Rosette Nebula (Figure 8.3). Lying about 5,000 light years distant from Earth (where one light year – despite the name! – is a distance of 9.5 million million

FIGURE 8.3. The cavity in the Rosette Nebula. A central cluster of young stars illuminates the layers of gas and dust in the nebula around them. Credit: NASA, the DSS-II and GSC-II Consortia.

kilometres; the distance that light travels in one year), this roughly spherical nebula spans around a hundred light years from one side to another. It is thus an immense structure, particularly when one considers that the Sun's nearest neighbour is around four light years away from us. A cluster of hot blue stars dominates the centre of the pink Rosette. These condensed from denser pockets of material within a diffuse cloud some four million years ago, and they now illuminate and heat the surrounding remnants of gas to give off hydrogen's characteristic pink glow. The young blue stars themselves inhabit a low-density cavity within the nebula, caused as their heat warmed the gas in the immediate vicinity so that it expanded and pushed back the surroundings to create a bubble. This effect is enhanced both by the radiation pressure of the stellar light (whereby energetic photons impart a push on matter) and by the physical winds of charged particles that stream continually from the surfaces of young stars. These both act to erode the walls of the newly formed cavity around the stars.

Introducing dust

Not only are there gas atoms occupying the space between the stars, but mixed in with the gas are small solid particles, called dust grains. With a characteristic size of around one micro-metre, these are about one-thousandth the width of a human hair, or the size of particles in cigarette smoke. The dust is made of carbonates (mostly in the form of graphite) and silicates – literally, soot and sand – and, if very cold, the grains can be coated with the frozen ice of water, ammonia or carbon dioxide. The total mass in such grains is only about one hundredth of that contained in all the stars. Despite the tiny grain size and low total mass, once collected into clouds that can stretch from tens to hundreds of light years across, the cumulative effect of the dust is sufficient to completely block the light from stars or gas clouds in the background. This effect is apparent from the striking dark rifts seen alongside the spiral arms of an external galaxy (Figure 8.2); as the dust clouds are largely confined to the plane of the disc, they block out so much light that a spiral galaxy seen edge-on can appear as if cut in two. Given that we live in the disc, we have an edge-on view of our own galaxy, which is why its stars are spread across the sky to form the band we call the Milky Way. The obscuration produced by the accompanying dust clouds is particularly pronounced in the southern hemisphere, where the night sky is directed towards the constellation of Sagittarius and the centre of our galaxy. Broad swathes of obscuration are apparent against the band of the Milky Way, and individual structures such as the Coalsack Nebula (close to the constellation of the Southern Cross) create large dark voids in the backdrop of stars.

The chemistry for the creation of dust grains requires a reasonably cool environment, such as that found in the extended outer layers of a star in a late stage of its evolution. The dust is then dispersed into the local interstellar medium when the star blows itself apart at the end of its life. The dust and gas coexist, with the grains embedded deep within the cold diffuse clouds; thus, the dust is another important component of nebulae. When dust is mixed with the cold gas in particularly dense concentrations, the high level of obscuration make such pockets appear as small opaque knots, known as globules, against the pink glimmer from the gas. The high density of dust grains in these small clouds not only prevents the light of the nearby stars from passing through the cloud, but the absorption also protects the core of the cloud from the stars' heat. Without an internal heat source, the temperature in the densest parts of the cloud can drop to only a few degrees above absolute zero. Under these conditions, the atoms in a cloud join up to form molecules on the surfaces of the grains – most commonly hydrogen, but also many more complex molecules such as water, ammonia and methanol. These *molecular clouds* have typical sizes from a few to fifty light years, and contain a mass of up to one thousand times that of the Sun. Although the molecular clouds are denser than, and embedded within, the diffuse clouds, they are still nowhere near as dense as the air that we breathe. In the images, the silhouettes of the dark globules very often show a jagged structure, which reveals how the light and winds from the nearby massive stars have a harsh corrosive effect that erodes from the outside.

One of the most familiar constellations in the winter sky is Orion the hunter, clearly marked out by some of the brightest stars in the sky. Far less obvious to stargazers is the fact that Orion also marks the direction of a giant diffuse cloud, some 1,500 light years away, that stretches from shoulder to toe across the constellation. Its most obvious manifestation is at the Great Orion Nebula, which marks the position of the hunter's sword, and is the only emission nebula visible to the unaided eye. The full extent of the complex network of nebulae in this region is only revealed in deep telescopic images taken through filters that emphasize the light from excited hydrogen gas. One famous example is the Horsehead Nebula, which sits just below and to the side of Alnitak, the lowest of the three stars that make up Orion's belt. In the visible waveband, the presence of a lurking dust cloud can be sensed by a sudden depopulation in the number of background stars and the luminous pink glow that is emitted by gas streaming away at the edge of the cloud irradiated by starlight. An outcropping of dense dusty material produces the silhouette of the eponymous horse's head (Figure 8.4). The topside of the Horsehead Nebula has a crisp edge, which shows where the stellar winds and radiation are steadily carving into the cloud at the *working surface*. To the left along this edge a bright glimmer reveals where a young star is breaking free from

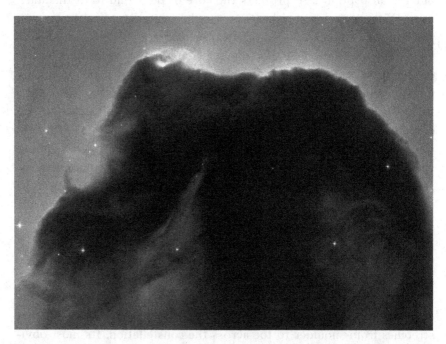

FIGURE 8.4. The top of the Horsehead Nebula. The 'Horsehead' is shaped from a cold dark cloud of gas and dust, illuminated by bright stars beyond the top of the image, which are also eroding gas at the top 'working edge' of the cloud. Stars seen through the cloud are clearly reddened in colour, and to the top left a new star is breaking free of its confines.
Credit: NASA, NOAO, ESA and The Hubble Heritage Team (STScI/AURA), with acknowledgement to K. Noll, C. Luginbuhl and F. Hamilton.

the cloud: a first indication that star formation is associated with the denser, dustier regions of a cloud.

The stars seen through the cloud appear much redder in colour than those viewed along clearer lines of sight to either side of the cloud. As it diminishes the light from background stars, dust also changes the colour of that light, making it redder, by a process of scattering. Photons can collide with particles of dust and cause them to deviate from their original path and travel in random directions. Light is scattered most efficiently by particles of a smaller size than its wavelength; the typical size of interstellar dust grains means that they are most effective at scattering the bluer (smaller) wavelengths. So when a star's light passes through a dusty cloud en route to the observer, the blue colours of this light are preferentially scattered away and no longer reach us. Only the redder portion of the starlight emerges from the other side of the cloud. This scattering is a similar process to that which gives us red sunrises and sunsets here on Earth. When it is close to the horizon, we observe the Sun through more of the dense portion of our atmosphere (that closer to the Earth's surface), which results in increased scattering by molecules of air, and the blue light is lost; this turns the Sun much redder than when it is at higher altitudes. The effect is enhanced when the atmosphere contains extra localized scattering particles, such as ash or dust. During the day we see all the blue light that is continually scattered out of sunlight in all directions as our sky. In the same way that this scattered blue light renders the atmosphere visible to us here on Earth, scattered blue light can also render a dust cloud visible. A bright star that is not hot enough to excite the gas atoms to glow can still have its blue light scattered by dust, to reveal the surrounding cloud as a distinctly blue *reflection nebula*. The obvious blue hue of the Pleiades is due not just to the colour of the forty to fifty stars that make up the young cluster, but also to the way that their light is scattered by a neighbouring dust cloud. Other stunning examples include the Iris Nebula, where a dusty cloud morphs from a veil of obscuration to a glowing blue ghost around a bright star, and the Witch's Head Nebula, which scatters blue light from the nearby bright star Rigel to reveal its distinctive profile.

Infrared radiation from dust

The dust can, however, also be detected directly. The energy of the absorbed photons raises the temperature of dust grains to a few tens or hundreds of degrees above absolute zero. Objects at this temperature (including humans!) radiate brightly at infrared wavelengths, and so do the grains of dust. Thus, dark obscuring clouds that block the light of stars in optical images are incandescent when observed with an infrared telescope and their inherent structures and shapes are revealed. Given that the longer (i.e. the redder) the wavelength of light the better it can travel through dust relatively unimpeded, any infrared light given off by stars tucked inside dusty clouds can escape – unlike visible radiation. Infrared observations can thus penetrate through a dusty cloud to reveal new clusters of stars that are still forming deep within the denser, obscured parts of a nebula. It is also through the infrared emission that we can verify both the origin of the dust and the presence of the molecules. One of the largest and most luminous known stars is VY Canis Majoris, a red supergiant star near the end of its life. It is currently ejecting huge quantities of material from its outer layers into interstellar space, forming a large extended cloud. The distribution of the colours of the infrared light emitted provides information on the properties of the dust grains that produce the broad-band radiation, and prominent spikes of infrared colour can be identified with many different molecules, particularly carbon monoxide and water.

Many of the most dramatic features within a nebula are caused by stellar winds and light pushing on the dust grains at the working edge of the nebula. The smaller, lighter dust particles exposed to this are pushed away most easily; the more massive particles or those that are embedded in the very dense concentrations are least affected and most resistant to erosion. Nowhere is this more evident than in the heart of the Eagle Nebula, 7,000 light years away in the next inner spiral arm of our Milky Way. A cluster of stars formed at the core of a large dusty cloud of gas some five million years ago and are now surrounded by a cavity with glowing walls of gas, which is excited by the radiation from the hot young stars. Pillars protrude from these walls, and all point inwards in the direction of the star cluster; the most famous of these are known affectionately as the 'pillars of creation' (Figure 8.1). These long tall towers of cold gas and dust rise up to heights of ten light years and show up in silhouette against the glow of the background gas emission. The shape of these towering pillars is a characteristic signature of the erosion process. The energetic ultraviolet radiation lights up the exposed surface of a cavity wall, and heats it so that sparse diffuse gas is boiled away. Strong stellar winds and radiation also push on all the matter, and this steady erosion is resisted only by the coldest, densest clumps of gas and dust. Remaining in place, they can provide shelter much like an umbrella, shielding the less dense regions behind them from the corrosive effects of the stars. Thus protected, long towers of gas are left in the shadow of the densest clumps, while their surroundings are steadily burnt away. Such dusty pillars can be found in all nebulae; the Horsehead is one (Figure 8.4) and less prominent examples can be seen to the top right of the Rosette Nebula (Figure 8.3). All point radially towards the source of the radiation (the stellar cluster at the centre of the nebula). Even smaller outcrops along the sides of the pillars are shaped to form fingers pointing in the same direction. At the very top of each pillar, exposed material is continually eroded until only the very densest pockets are left behind to eventually break free and float as individual dense globules. Several can be seen escaping from the top of the left-most pillar in the Eagle Nebula (Figure 8.1). Each globule is much wider than the Solar System, and they provide the next step in the story of nebulae. To see where they lead us, we must move to the Great Orion Nebula in the sword of Orion, where a variety of similar features at a later stage of their development can be observed.

Star birth

The Orion Nebula is one of the greatest local star formation regions, 'only' 1,600 light years away from us. It was created when a star cluster carved out a cavity that has broken through the nearside edge of a dark molecular cloud, enabling us to peer inside. Infrared observations reveal thick layers of surrounding dust that hides the presence of at least a thousand very young stars. Imaging of the immediate environs of the most prominent of these – the Trapezium of stars well known to amateur observers – reveals isolated small dark globules with a flattened egg shape. They are seen either as opaque silhouettes against the bright hydrogen gas emission, or sometimes illuminated by the young stars. These dusty cocoons are the next stage in the development of the blobs that are evident in the Eagle Nebula and are left behind when all of the lighter, fluffier material around them was eroded away. Each cocoon has a size several times that of the Solar System. Denser than their surroundings, they are in the process of collapsing inwards under gravity and are becoming steadily more concentrated and thus opaque to visible light. Infrared observations that can peer into the cocoons show many to contain a single proto-star buried deep at the core: these dusty globules are where stars are born. As matter falls together under gravity at the very core of the cocoon, it gains energy and heats up; as more and more matter is accreted, the central condensation can reach temperatures of some millions of degrees. At this point the material at the centre is hot enough to commence nuclear fusion – the energy-producing process that powers a star and enables it to resist the further inward pull of gravity. A proto-star is formed, and soon it begins to pour out a combination of light, heat, jets and winds that will eventually break through the imme-diate surroundings to reveal the newly born star to the outside universe.

The formation of the star does not use all of the matter that constitutes its nest; it does not need to accrete all of the cloud to reach sufficient temperature to switch on. The remaining dusty material surrounds the star and forms a ring-shaped proto-planetary disc – or *proplyd*, a very early stage in the formation of a planetary system. When such proplyds were first discovered (in the mid-1990s) around many of the newly forming stars in Orion, it was the first concrete evidence that planetary systems around stars other than our Sun could be common. (Certainly, we believe that our own Solar System formed from a cocoon such as these, some 4.5 billion years ago.) A proplyd is shaped into a flat disc because it is not stationary. A globule will inherit any incipient rotation inherent in its parent cloud. The rotation speed is greatly amplified as it shrinks in size due to gravitational collapse, and the spinning mass of the cloud flattens out. The star at the core of the proplyd will be formed as a spinning body. As the proto-star begins to radiate, it erodes the cocoon and morphs it into a thick ring of gas and dust that will – over the next hundred million years or so – evolve into the accompanying planets. Whether the proplyds we observe in Orion will form planetary systems that really resemble our own is far less certain. The high-resolution images show that they are suffering heavy erosion from the outside as well. The energetic radiation and winds given off by the massive young stars forming the Trapezium are pushing on the gas and dust of the proplyds, shaping them more like wind socks or comet tails that stream away from the source of the blast. The outer layers of the proplyds are stripped such that any planetary systems formed would be made up of only a tight core of planets wrapped around their host sun.

Star death

Clearly the nebulae that we study reveal much about the connection between the interstellar medium and the formation of stars. But nebulae are, of course, also intimately associated with stars at the other end of their life cycles. Once a star has ignited at the centre of a cocoon, the whole of its existence is a battle against the inevitable inward pull of gravity. It supports itself against its collapse by fusing atomic nuclei of relatively low mass together, in a long and complicated chain of nuclear reactions. In this way the star both gradually stockpiles nuclei of much greater mass and obtains a source of internal energy to make it shine and to resist gravity. This continues until the star effectively runs out of appropriate fuel, which then leaves gravity to claim its victory. What happens to the star at that point depends mainly upon its mass.

Planetary nebulae

A star with a mass similar to that of our Sun can live for about ten billion years before the fuel supplies at its very core are depleted. There are various stages within its life cycle: while it spends most of its time most simply burning hydrogen to helium, in later years it swells to become a *red giant*. The star is not sufficiently massive or hot, however, to proceed significantly with the further fusion processes that produce more energy and create heavier elements. As the nuclear fusion dies away the gravity of the star begins to squeeze the inner core, causing it to collapse rapidly and heat up again as it does so. The collapse is halted when the outward pressure produced by the motion of the electrons in the densely packed material is enough to resist gravity, and the core forms a *white dwarf*. During its initial collapse the sharp increase in the core's temperature rapidly heats the outer layers of the star, and they are driven away in an outward wind, to form a surrounding bubble-like shell known as a *planetary nebula*. The uncovered white dwarf at its centre will eventually cool and fade over many millions of years, but in the mean time its radiation heats and excites the gases in the nebula. The atoms in the shell glow and are visible as beautiful bubble-like structures. One of the simplest is the Ring Nebula (Figure 8.5), an easy target for the amateur astronomer, which lies in the constellation of Lyra. The spherical shell formed from the outer layers is illuminated by the compact white dwarf clearly seen as a white dot at the centre. Faint radial fingers of obscuration can be seen mixed in with the gas: these are composed of the dust that was formed during the star's final red giant phase and later thrown in the outer layers of its atmosphere. A planetary nebula is relatively transitory – as it expands it will disperse into space over a period of several thousand years, cooling down and fading as it does so.

While visible, such structures provide the opportunity for the observation and modelling of processes that can occur during the last few thousand years in the life of a Sun-like star. Few are as simple as the Ring Nebula. Some show far more intricate structures, such as the complex webbing apparent in the Spirograph Nebula, or the bipolar lobes that spread out from the white dwarf to form the suitably named Hourglass, Ant or Butterfly Nebulae. One of the most complex planetary nebulae known is the famous Cat's Eye, which is shaped from ten concentric gas shells that were blown off in a sequence of regular pulses at 1,500-year intervals. The regular pattern of shells is disturbed by the passage of two high-velocity jets and wind bubbles that emerged later from the dying star. As with many of these nebulae, a wider-angle view reveals much larger, very faint haloes of matter thrown off at far earlier episodes of the star's evolution, some five to ten thousand years previously. Certainly it would appear that many stars do not end their lives in a simple spherically symmetric 'textbook' manner. Planetary nebulae may also have the development of

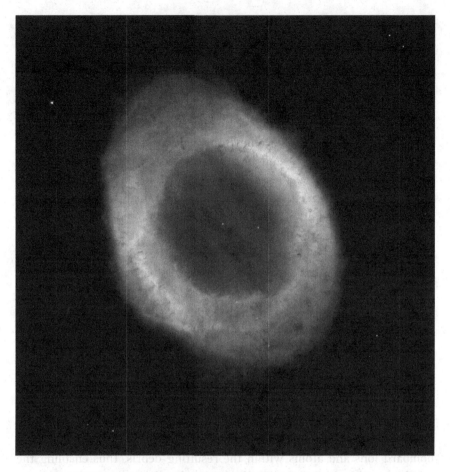

FIGURE 8.5. The Ring Nebula. The Ring Nebula is a planetary nebula, a shell formed from the outer layers of a star, shed at the end of its life, and expanding away into space. The central core of the dying star is a white dwarf, which can be seen as a white dot at the centre of the ring. The whole structure is about one light year across.
Credit: The Hubble Heritage Team (AURA/STScI/NASA).

their structures influenced by any dusty layers shrugged off by the star earlier on, which can produce an inhomogeneous environment that moulds an asymmetric expansion of the gas layers. Shapes can also be complicated by the presence of a close companion star or strong magnetic fields contained within the expelled material.

Supernova remnants

Much more massive stars (around eight times the mass of our Sun) have a very different life. With more mass comes far more gravity to be overpowered, so the star has to produce far more outward energy from the nuclear fusion. This requires it to undergo a much higher rate of fusion processes at much higher temperatures. In the real world of physics – in contrast to the common perception of blue as 'cold' and red as 'hot' – hotter objects emit bluer, more energetic radiation than the yellowy-red colour of cooler stars such as our Sun. Thus an astronomer immediately recognizes that any blue stars in an image are both massive and very hot. In addition, blue stars can always be identified as young stars. Producing more energy, they consume fuel at a much faster rate. Even though they start with far more mass, the rapidity with which it is devoured means that stars with a mass over ten times that of our Sun only live for some tens of millions of years. The more massive the star, the shorter its lifetime. A convoluted chain of nuclear reactions can be supported at these much higher temperatures, which results in the core of the star being completely converted to much heavier elements, up to and including iron. Once a star has created iron (the most tightly bound nucleus) it can no longer extract energy via fusion, and it abruptly runs out of power. The final collapse from gravity is rapid and dramatic, and results in a complete disruption of the star in a *supernova* explosion. During this disruption an intense flood of neutrons is released, and these bombard ions and atoms within the resulting debris, thus enabling the rapid formation of elements much heavier than iron.

When a much higher mass (and hence higher gravity) drives the collapse of the star, the atoms in the core are squeezed beyond the point where electron pressure is sufficient to resist gravity. Within each atom, electrons are now forced onto protons to create neutrons, and the incompressibility of this population of neutrons can hold up the star against further collapse. The remnant core comes to rest as an incredibly dense, and tiny, neutron star. But if the mass in the original giant star exceeded twenty-five solar masses, it is a completely different story. The final gravitational collapse of the core pushes past the neutron pressure, and there is no process that can any longer support the star. The matter in the core will continue falling inwards under gravity, and turn it into one of the oddest objects in the Universe: a black hole.

The supernova explosion blasts off the outer layers of the star to generate a tide of debris, which expands away at over half a million kilometres an hour. The rapidly moving shell of matter sweeps up the surrounding interstellar medium, compressing and collapsing the material in front of it into thin sheets and filaments. Shocks are generated as the blast-wave collides with its environs, and the energy that is released heats the gas in the filaments to temperatures of millions of degrees. As this material in the shell cools, the atoms radiate away the energy and trace a filigree network of filaments up to hundreds of light years across. Such a supernova remnant remains visible long after the initial explosion and can persist for tens of thousands of years. The Crab Nebula (Figure 8.6) is the nearby (6,500 light years from Earth) remnant of a supernova explosion that was recorded as a bright 'guest star' by Chinese astronomers over a thousand years ago. Today the shreds of debris form a cloud around 10 light years in diameter, still expanding from the centre at over 1,000 kilometres a second.

During this process, all of the heavier elements created – whether during the massive star's life or at its violent death – become mixed in with the primordial gas of the interstellar medium and subtly enrich its chemical composition. But it is these same diffuse gas clouds, now seeded with a trace of heavy elements, that will one day collapse to form another generation of new stars. As the history of the Galaxy proceeds, subsequent generations of star birth and death have a cumulative effect, slowly increasing the proportion of heavy elements present. The interstellar medium is dynamic, with star birth and death occurring all of the time, very often in close proximity. Any given nebula will be dominated by a cluster of young massive stars sitting in the cavity they have created around them. Their radiation is eroding the walls of the molecular hydrogen cloud around them to form giant dusty pillars and in the process isolating small dark globules, some of which are already collapsing into proplyds around proto-stars. The most massive stars of a cluster are the first to explode as a supernova, and the heavy elements that they release will become incorporated into future generations of

FIGURE 8.6. The Crab Nebula. The Crab Nebula is a six-light-year-wide nebula formed from the debris of a massive star's supernova explosion that occurred around a thousand years ago. The central core of the star has collapsed down to form a neutron star at the centre of the nebula.
Credit: NASA, ESA, J. Hester and A. Loll (Arizona State University).

stars to be born out of this cloud. In this way, all of the heavy chemical elements that form the Earth and our bodies were originally created deep in the heart of massive stars, many billions of years ago. Sometimes the supernova blast is even responsible for triggering the next generation of stars.

The triggers for star formation

We observe star formation to be ongoing throughout the disc of our Galaxy. But many of these gas clouds are primordial and have existed for billions of years. What causes them to collapse to form stars only now? To understand this, we have to examine how and why the process of star formation starts.

Every atom or molecule in a gas cloud is pulled on by the combined gravitational attraction of its neighbouring particles. The slightest over-density of matter in a diffuse cloud will make the gravity slightly stronger in one location, and as this over-density condenses, its increased mass results in an increased gravitational pull on its surroundings, which in turn attracts more matter, so it becomes denser, more massive and gravitationally stronger ... and so a runaway process of gravitational collapse is triggered. Gravity squeezes the matter tighter and hotter until the point where nuclear fusion – and thus star birth – is triggered. But all matter in a gas cloud, even if it is only a few degrees above absolute zero, is in continuous motion. The constant jiggling and movement of particles produces a net outward pressure, which, if large enough, enables the particles in a cloud to resist the local pull of its own gravity. So whether or not a cloud of a certain size will collapse to form stars is dictated by a delicate balance between its density and temperature. A threshold density is required to overcome the thermal pressure, and this threshold is higher the warmer the cloud. (There are other factors, such as the strength of any magnetic field threading through the gas, or the amount of rotation present, that can also act to inhibit a cloud's collapse under gravity.) Thus the conditions for star formation are most favourable in the very coolest and densest regions of the interstellar medium, such as the cold dusty globules. There are many invisible cold gas clouds that have not collapsed yet – they can exist undisturbed for hundreds of millions of years if the material in them is either too sparse or too hot to condense spontaneously under gravity. Either the temperature or the density of the cloud has to change substantially to cause it to collapse to form stars. A rapid decrease in temperature across portions of a cloud is nearly impossible to effect, but a quick increase in density can be achieved by a variety of physical processes, all of which can push on the gas and squeeze it.

Star formation is endemic throughout the flat disc of our Galaxy, as evinced by the plethora of blue-star clusters. The exact source of the spiral pattern is not well understood, but it is thought to be due to a 'density wave' that slowly sweeps round the disc, perhaps caused by the way that gas clouds will occasionally bunch together as they rotate around the centre of the Galaxy. The density wave squeezes the gas clouds as it passes, triggering star formation and leaving a long arc of newly formed star clusters in its wake. Compression of gas clouds can exist on smaller, more local, scales as well. The winds and radiation streaming from the surface of very young stars hollow out a cavity – either round an individual massive star, or a combined effort around a cluster of stars such as those in the Rosette Nebula (Figure 8.3). The material excavated piles up to form a thick layer and in the process is compressed, which makes the cavity walls an ideal location for a new region of star birth. The infrared images clearly show large, embryonic stars within these walls, and, in particular, stars located deep inside the tips of the pillars that branch from them.

One of the best examples of a nebula that shows three successive generations of star formation is the Heart and Soul Nebula, a structure that spans 300 light years, around 6,500 light years away. The ages of the stars are observed as systematically younger with increasing distance from the centre of the 'Soul' side of the nebula. Isolated blue stars seen right at the centre of the large cavity are the only remaining survivors from the first clusters of stars to form from the surrounding molecular cloud – any more massive companions have long since lived out their lives. Some young star clusters lie further from the centre: these are a second generation that were prompted to collapse from the compression of gas clouds by the winds, radiation pressure and subsequent supernova blast waves from the original star clusters. Many of the stars in these clusters are accompanied by (rather wind-blown) proplyds. Finally, infrared observations reveal a third generation of young stars and proto-stars, all still embedded within the cavity walls and towering dust pillars. In this way, a dynamic cycle of star birth and star death ripples out from the core of a nebula, enriching and triggering subsequent generations.

Final comment

This chapter has discussed images that many people find both beautiful and awe-inspiring, which were all created from data collected in the pursuit of scientific knowledge; I hope that a better explanation of the underlying science has only enhanced their beauty in the eye of the beholder.

Acknowledgements

There are many more beautiful images of star clusters and nebulae available for the reader to explore and marvel at, all created from the observations of both professional and amateur astronomers around the world. These continue to provide inspiration for my own fascination for astronomy. Two suggestions of starter websites for the interested reader are the Astronomy Picture of the Day at *apod.nasa.gov* and the Heritage Gallery of *Hubble Space Telescope* images at *heritage.stsci.edu.*

Index

Index